FEATHER
THE PERFECT PORTABLE®

And Its Stitches Across History

NANCY JOHNSON-SREBRO

with

Technical Assistance by Frank Srebro

Exclusive Distributor:

C&T Publishing, Inc.
P.O. Box 1456
Lafayette, CA 94549
800.284.1114
www.ctpub.com

Published By:

Silver Star, Inc.
55 Saddle Lake Rd.
Tunkhannock, PA 18657

ISBN 978-1-60705-263-0

Printed in China

20 19 18 17 16 15 14 13 12

FOREWORD

I started looking for *Featherweights* over seven years ago. But my desire to own one got the best of me in the Fall of 1990. I'd just returned from the AIQA Festival in Houston. While I was teaching there several *Featherweights* had slipped through my fingers, and I was, to say the least, disappointed! A day or two later my husband asked what I wanted for Christmas, and I said I really wanted to see a black case with an old *Featherweight* under the tree. He asked if I was kidding, and I assured him I wasn't. Well Frank usually isn't held back by much but I have to admit the poor guy barely knew what a *Featherweight* was at the time. I found out later that he started the search right then and there. Two weeks before Christmas he was able to buy not one, but two machines. And when I raced to the tree that year I saw that Santa had left two black cases!

It's been over four years since I wrote the first edition of this book, and my respect and love for these wonderful sewing machines continue to grow. With the help of many people I've been able to gather a large mass of new information on the *Featherweight Model 221.* Armed with hundreds of letters, phone messages and personal notes, I felt it was time to write again about the Perfect Portable. I must say, though, without the help of my husband I would never have been able to take on a project of this size. Frank spent months cataloging my research, and entering this information and my book manuscript into one of our computers. Actually, I've written this book update on a parallel path along with another book on quiltmaking.

I decided early-on to divide this book up and organize it so it would not be too repetitious, but yet make each chapter fairly complete for those readers who skip chapters on subjects that don't interest them. I think you'll find that each chapter has a "stand alone" character that doesn't depend heavily on information in preceding sections.

As a quilt teacher and a quilting book author, I've seen literally thousands of *Singer Featherweight 221* sewing machines in classes and seminars across the country. There's no doubt that the classic *Featherweight 221* portable carries more prestige in quilting class than any other sewing machine. "Charisma" might be a good word to use here. And for good reasons! A classic should have at least one special virtue. *Featherweights* have many. It's no wonder they've become an important part of the resurgence of the quilt making art in this country. We all have seen this happen - a legend made in our time! I'm happy to have been a part of it, and I'm sure you are too!

So it's with great pleasure that we present to you our updated volume of Featherweight 221 - The Perfect Portable. Enjoy!

DEDICATION

Maybe it was God's providence, or call it coincidence if you will, but the very day I finished the manuscript for this edition I received a letter that touched my heart. A woman in Texas told me about her friend who used to buy *Featherweights* for her business. She had one machine to which a note was attached in a very shaky hand. It said "I hope whoever gets this machine will love it as much as I have".

Here's a salute to you, my unknown friend, for phrasing so well what's taken long months and pages and pages to capture. And let me dedicate this modest work to you . . . . I promise that you and your machine will be remembered.

ACKNOWLEDGMENTS

Books such as this one result from the assistance and support of many people. Foremost among these contributors is the Singer Sewing Company of Edison, New Jersey, and its Sewing Product Department personnel. I am grateful for their assistance with product and technical information which was invaluable in the preparation of this work.

One individual stands well at the head of my list of new *Featherweight* friends: Dale Pickens of Oklahoma. Dale has been a friend since the first edition of this book hit the market. And he's shared much technical information since then, helping to sharpen my perspective for some sections of this new edition.

Other individuals who deserve recognition for letters, information and support in the production of this work include the following: Christina Bertrand, NY; Bruce Chapman, MA; Ronald Collins, VT; Tom Corn, Jr., MO; Ruth Edsall, N.S.; Joseph Fitzpatrick, ME; Francis Gibson, MD; Megan Griffiths, N.Z.; Roger Allan Hamstreet, VA; Sally Heaton, OH; Edward Hetzel, PA; Gail Hinson, CA; Bill Holman, WI; Mary Jablonowski, PA; Robert Johnston, KS; Angela Jones, CA; Shon Jones, IA; Jean Kullberg, AZ; Paul Maria, PA; Tom Martin and Marjorie McBride, CA; Norma McGara, TX; Marguerite Newell, N.S.; JoAnn Overton, NY; Grace Marie Patane, NY; Barb and Les Perrin, MI; Alice Polk, CA; Donna and Arnold Poster, TX; Vivian Proctor, TX; Frank Pucello, CA; Carole and Jim Richardson, OR; Marilyn Root, OH; Donna Sanders, WI; Maury Anne Sanders, AL; Kristina and Bob Santilla, MD; Barb Sawyer, TX; Roy Schulte, MI; James Slaten, CA; Violet Stewart, N.Z.; E. Russell Tarleton, WA; Floyd Turley, OK; Jacqueline Van Voris, MA; Pat Williams, MI; Gerri and Bob Wootten, TX

List of Trademarks

Author's Note

Special note should be taken by the reader that the name "*Featherweight*" and the "*Model 221*" designation are promotional and descriptive references that were used by the *Singer Sewing Company* to designate a particular portable sewing machine and its variants that were manufactured and sold, worldwide, between about 1933-70. I have freely substituted these terms and used them interchangeably throughout this book.

Warranty

CONTENTS

FEATHERWEIGHT 221
THE PERFECT PORTABLE ™
INTRODUCTION

Quite possibly the best known, most interesting and sought-after American sewing machine of all time is the *Singer Model 221 Featherweight*. A "breakthrough" machine when born, it was a winner from the start. The *Featherweight* represented a successful effort by a great and famous company to meet its customers' needs. You can trace the flow and ebb, the changes of taste, in its history. And the *Model 221* just plain refuses to die! Even today, some twenty seven years since it left the line, the Perfect Portable is more popular than ever with a new generation of quilt makers, seamstresses and collectors. This book will help you appreciate, find and use this wonderful and beloved portable sewing machine.

Singer® Featherweight Model 221's

CHAPTER ONE

PERSPECTIVES

I t had no cams nor computer circuitry. It wasn't offered in designer colors. It didn't do fancy stitching, not even a zigzag. It wasn't made as a fancy, prestige model. It was lightweight when heavyweights dominated the field. It wasn't cheap, nor was it outrageously expensive. But . . . . it was self-contained, and it didn't need a host of technical experts to fix it. And it was compact and easy to store away. Salesmen ran it while balanced on its attachment box, set on edge, and it wouldn't fall off. It had a reliability that was second to none. It would become the standard by which all portables were judged - the benchmark. They called it the Perfect Portable, possibly the finest lightweight sewing machine on the market. They predicted you could use it for a lifetime, give it to your daughter and then to her daughter.

"They" are the three generations of American women who have used and loved the *Singer Featherweight 221* sewing machine, and everything they said about it is true. As I write this in 1997, some twenty seven years after it left the factory lineup, *Featherweights* are in the highest demand ever, especially by quilt makers. Sewing machine dealers can sell a trade-in without even putting it on the shelf, and waiting lists of years are the rule. In short, the *Singer Featherweight 221* has become a legend.

Being a rather plain-Jane, no frills sort of sewing machine, you may wonder why the *Featherweight* has garnered such a respectable following in our times of ever-sophisticated models by many manufacturers. Even though we're close to the turn of the millennium and computers all but control our lives, some say this nineteen-thirties throwback has become an absolutely integral part of modern quilt making. But, to understand, put yourself back into the time frame of the thirties. During that conservative decade, an original was born. It was very different than the norm, yet it fit in so perfectly that it became the standard, the one to remember and even to imitate. Originals become classics as they stand the test of time. And so it is with the *Featherweight*. Today's *Featherweight* scene is a kaleidoscope of the machines and the people who have, and do own them. As long as women persist in pursuing fabric arts, and loving quilts in particular, I believe the legendary *Singer Featherweight* sewing machine will be with us.

CHAPTER TWO

THE BEGINNING

By the late 1920's the words "sewing machine" meant *Singer* to most women. It was (and is) a standout company, well established throughout the country. Competitors abounded; but *Singer* had the name, it had the products, and it had the marketing. The customers followed. Despite the women's liberation of the Roaring Twenties era, sewing machine demand was steady. Basic sewing and mending were necessary in most every household, and many women continued to challenge themselves with more creative projects.

Treadle machines were on their way out, and the new electrics had hit the marketplace with both feet running. In today's age of microwave ovens, home computers and TV remotes, an electric motor may seem passé. But in the nineteen twenties and thirties, when rural America was being electrified, the convenience of a small, simple motor was awesome! The early electric machines were mainly sewing heads that were designed for treadle operation, but with the addition of a motor and its foot or knee speed controller. Innovations quickly appeared, and before long the electric machines on the market had been engineered from the ground up. Weight wasn't a big design factor, because machine heads were more or less permanently installed in a cabinet in the home. Even the early portables were not much more than standard heads that came with a base, cover and carrying handle.

Enter the *Standard Sewing Machine Company* of Cleveland, Ohio, with the first truly portable machine named the *Sewhandy*. It only weighed 12 pounds and it was gear driven throughout, with all rotary motion. It had many advanced features such as a built-in motor, sewing light, and a fully enclosed lower drive. And it was small and self-contained. The company's advertisement said it came in an "attractive case of washable leatherette material (that) measures only 13 inches its longest way". Mechanically, the *Sewhandy* was well balanced, which was not necessary with heavy cast iron machine heads. It would operate on a kitchen table or a convenient shelf without "walking" around. Standard even advertised that "Your *Sewhandy* and a card table are all you need to do your sewing in the sunny room at any hour of the day". Looking backwards from today, the machine, its carrying case and the card table reference were nothing short of a prophecy. Little did *Standard's* marketing and engineering management know that they had brilliantly foreseen a product need that was coming up in the dark days ahead. And they had set the stage for the upcoming *Featherweight Model 221* - the Perfect Portable!

Standard Sewhandy

The Stock Market Crash of 1929, and the Great Depression that followed, had an impact on most everything in American life. Tight money forced more women to the sewing machine, and machines were finally offered with a reverse sewing feature - for darning and mending. Although this was an early invention, it was not widely offered to the home sewing machine buyer prior to that period of hard times. Apparently the manufacturers did

13

not think it would sell very well. The lack of work caused families to move about, and the vignette of the old jalopy loaded with everything but the kitchen sink was repeated all too frequently all over the country. Store sales slowed down, and Singer even introduced a new marketing concept - with a car, trailer and sales team - to bring the store out to the customers. Sewing machines were demonstrated by powering from a bank of 6 volt batteries wired together. The tragic dust storms of 1934 and 1935 completed the ruin for untold numbers of farmers. Families started migrating toward the Golden West, and California in particular - El Dorado was always westward. The need for a reliable, truly portable sewing machine had come to pass.

It seems that the *Standard Sewing Machine Company* was a casualty of the Depression, selling out to a successor, the *Ossan Manufacturing Company* - a sad commentary on the economics of the times. One of my references puts this in 1929. *Standard* had been in business since 1880, advertising itself as "Manufacturers of High Grade Sewing Machines for Home Use". *Ossan* reportedly manufactured the *Sewhandy* for a period, selling out, in turn, to *Singer* only two years later in 1931. To confuse matters a bit for *Sewhandy* collectors, the *General Electric Company* of Bridgeport, Connecticut, was also involved with the Sewhandy somewhere in this time frame. G. E. did manufacture the motors for the *Standard Sewhandy* but it also began to sell the machine under its own name as the "Model A". I suspect this was a licensing arrangement with either *Standard* or *Ossan*, but despite quite a bit of research I haven't been able to figure out who licensed it. Adding to this confusion is the Instruction Booklet for the *General Electric* version: it uses much of the same text, and some of the same photos and illustrations as in the Standard Sewhandy booklet! Apparently the marketing arrangement allowed this use. I've noted also that some of the Model A's are heavier than the original *Sewhandy*. The heavy ones have beds made of iron rather than aluminum, weighing about 3 pounds more, or about 15 pounds ready to sew.

Carole and Jim Richardson

G.E. Sewhandy Model A

All told, I believe the *Sewhandy* was the immediate predecessor of the *Featherweight*, or at least it strongly influenced its design. There are just too many similarities between the two machines. This conjecture on my part has been supported by many correspondents, but disputed by others. One man from Iowa wrote to me about the *Singer* Class 24-80 Portable Electric Chain Stitch machine, suggesting it inspired the *Featherweight*. After looking into this, I don't think it was a major influence. The 24-80 is a chain stitch machine, it doesn't use a bobbin, it has no tension adjustments and it's mainly intended for use on delicate fabrics. Remember these features, and consider a story I heard from a former *Singer* salesman in Vermont. Early in his career he made a call on a woman who used her *Featherweight* for 25 years sewing on braided rugs; she finally wore out the drive belt! Yes, the 24-80 is a small portable electric machine, and it does have a carrying case that resembles the *Featherweight's* case. But that's where the similarity ends.

Singer's engineers kept the Sewhandy's desirable features, and added significant improvements to the basic mechanism. And their production people took their usual special pains to build it right. This was the age of the craftsman. Officially named its Model 221, the new Featherweight made its debut at the 1933 World's Fair in Chicago, and this is one of the interesting paradoxes around the Featherweight. The midst of the Depression was an odd and risky time to introduce a new, revolutionary model of anything; but there was a need and Singer must have felt that there was some money out there. Think about it! People were standing in food lines and hundreds of men would compete for every job. The wheels of industry were barely creaking along. How much demand should there have been for new sewing machines, no less a model that looked like a toy as compared with most other machines in the showrooms? But something very different was born, and it fit in perfectly. It should have flopped, but it didn't. Singer's Featherweight caught on, built its reputation, and the little marvel endured.

Mowry Photo

Singer® Model 221 Featherweight

CHAPTER THREE

THE FEATHERWEIGHT NAME

I've been intrigued by the name *Featherweight* ever since I first heard it in the early '70s. To me, the word conjures up an image of something well beyond lightweight. "Ultra light" might be about right. Much later, when I began quilt teaching in earnest, I heard of the *Singer Featherweight*. I immediately assumed that the machine was a lightweight version of a regular model. But when I first saw one, I was shocked; the machine fit my original image perfectly! At 11 pounds, 1 ounce (5.0 kg) the *Singer Featherweight* is indeed ultra light. And there is only a slight resemblance to the standard head models of its day. It's really in a class by itself. It's no wonder quilt makers who travel to classes are combing the countryside to find the occasional machine that's for sale.

As a sidelight, my curiosity about multiple use of the Featherweight name led me to do some research on the subject. In 1996, the North American trademarks database, which includes Canada, and the federal and state databases, had a total of sixty three Featherweight trademark records, covering such goods as ball-point pens, diaries, sunglasses, and many other diverse products. Apparently, the name has been used often. As I expected, *Featherweight* is registered to *The Singer Company* with respect to sewing machines.

A final curiosity - one of my correspondents in Missouri sent along a copy of a page from a White Sewing Machine Company publication that refers to their Model 77MG machine - which was described as: the "Featherweight Portable type in the Luggage Case". It even looks a bit like the regular *Singer* Model 221. Unfortunately, the page is not dated, but from the text it appears to be from the late 40's or early 50's. I did some detective work. The basic White model 77 machine was made from 1946 to 1953, and was colored brown. I'll write more on this in a later chapter. It could be that the legend of the brown (Singer) *Featherweight* started with this machine and it's name.

CHAPTER FOUR

DESIGN FEATURES

I'll start this section with an illustration of a typical *Featherweight* machine for reference in the text that follows.

FEATHERWEIGHT 221 (TYPICAL MACHINE)

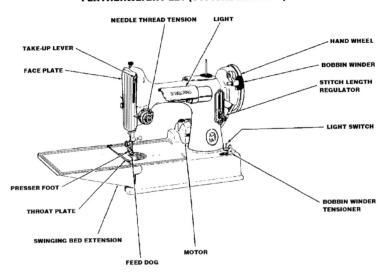

The Sewhandy Machine:

As I wrote previously, the *Sewhandy* was an innovation when it came on the market. It was first available in several proprietary colors: marine blue, larch green and ashes of roses. Black was added to the line later. Sales lasted until about 1931 when *Singer* bought *Ossan*. By 1933, Singer had time to study the pluses and minuses of the *Sewhandy*. One of its far-sighted design features was the concept of using a single piece of metal for both the machine bed and its lower housing. *Sewhandys* were totally self-contained and didn't require a separate base or cabinet

to enclose the shafts, gears and other gizmos beneath the machine -
all of the things we have to oil from time to time. Actually, its bed
was made of aluminum, like an inverted cake baking pan; and there
was enough space inside for the machinery I mentioned. A piece of
walnut-finished plywood provided access for oiling and maintenance,
and it was attached by several machine screws. The advantages of
this design were that the Sewhandy was self-contained, and it was
small and light (12 pounds/5.4 kg.).

The Featherweight inherited this basic design from the
Sewhandy. However, *Singer's* engineers greatly improved it
by adding a swinging bed extension or platform, to increase the
sewing surface to the left of its needle. It may seem like a simple
concept today, but this bed extension was a stroke of design genius
at the time. It proved to be immensely valuable to women who
piece large sections of fabric such as quilt tops. In addition, a thin
metal cover plate was provided on the bottom of the machine for
lubrication and maintenance of the lower bed mechanism. This
cover plate was held on by a single thumb nut, and it had a
gasket to prevent oil and grease leakage onto the table or work.
In comparison, the *Sewhandy* had several remote "oil holes"
located in strategic places on its bed surface. Direct application
of oil or grease to the lower drive was tedious - its wooden bottom
cover had to be removed, and a good size screwdriver was needed
to remove the four machine screws that held it in place. Also, you
had to unscrew the two tiny screws that held its sewing light and
wires (small screwdriver), and carefully move everything through
a small hole in its bed. Needless to say, oiling was mostly done by
using the oil holes . . . . if and when the owner remembered to do it.
This thought really hit me when I saw that the (circa 1932) *General
Electric* version of the machine had more oiling places than the
earliest versions of the *Sewhandy*.

Oil holes are prone to blockage due to fabric dust and lint,
which keeps oil from reaching the bearing and sliding surfaces
in the lower bed. I believe this accounts in part for the low
survival rate of Sewhandys . Before I wrote the original version
of this book in 1992, I'd seen only one Sewhandy machine in all
of my quilt teaching travels. And I bought it, mainly for research.

It was made in late 1928 by *Standard*, and it had a relatively low serial number. Since then I've seen more *Sewhandy* machines, but none had high serial numbers. From this limited production data I have concluded that *Sewhandys* were only moderately popular. It may have been that the machine was a bit ahead of its time.

Let me sum up. It seems that relatively few *Sewhandys* were sold, and its oiling design was not up to par. Both factors account for the relative scarcity of the machines today. As I write this book update in 1997, there are over seven hundred letters or notes in my files from folks who have written to me since my first edition was released. Of this total, only eighteen relate to *Sewhandy* machines; the vast majority refer in some manner to *Featherweights*.

As a sidelight here, let me say that the *Sewhandy* machines (whether *Standard, Ossan,* or *General Electric* variants) do not currently command the prestige factor nor the monetary value of a Featherweight. Ah, you say, but the *Sewhandy* machines are a lot scarcer than the common *Featherweights*, so they should be worth more. Oh, really? The supply and demand principle seems to apply here. Granted, the number of good, running *Sewhandys* is very low . . . . they are rarely found. But a high demand just isn't there, at least not as I write this. In recent years, quilt making has come back like an avalanche, and many thousands of quilters are looking for Featherweights. Unfortunately, the present demand for good Sewhandys seems to be from the limited number of folks who collect antique sewing machines for their footprints in history.

Other Improvements

This section summarizes the many improvements designed into the *Featherweight* machine. *Singer* stayed with aluminum as the material of construction for its new Model 221, but expanded its use to include the machine arm. This was a definite improvement over the use of cast iron in the *Sewhandy's* arm, because it compensated for the extra weight of the swinging bed extension, which was added. It's interesting to note that the *Featherweight* wasn't *Singer's* first sewing machine that made extensive use of lightweight aluminum. It's only about one-third as heavy as cast iron. Although it wasn't as cheap nor commonly used in the 1930's as today, it was available to their engineers. For perspective, I have a *Singer* brochure dated 1925 that advertised their "new model that was designed and built especially for electric motor operation, the *Singer* No. 101". This was a horizontal rotary hook machine that had a cast iron head of "large size and rigid construction (which) would be too heavy for use as a portable machine". Reading on, I found reference to the No. 101-10, a version made of aluminum. To quote further: "This problem (too heavy) has been solved by the use of aluminum for all of the heavy parts, such as the arm and bed. The savings in weight thus affected makes the complete outfit easily portable, weighing only 31 pounds". With tongue in cheek, I have to admit that I was tempted to highlight the words "only 31 pounds" in the last quotation. Times do change; today I can't imagine lugging around the equivalent of (six) five pound bags of sugar in one hand, and calling it easy. Remember, though, this was before the introduction of the new *Featherweight*. On a table or shelf, ready to sew, a *Model 221* weighed only slightly more than 11 pounds.

Another design improvement for the *Featherweight* was a reverse sewing feature. The *Sewhandy* didn't have one. This feature answered the need for darning and back tacking capability that had come with the hard times of the Great Depression. The *Model 221* also had a stitch length regulator that was well labeled and fully adjustable between 6 to 30 stitches to the inch. This improved on the *Sewhandy's* adjustment which was only marked off in arbitrary increments from numbers 1 through 6. Its owner had to remember what the numbers meant to set her desired stitch length.

Its rotary hook design was retained from the *Sewhandy*. It seems that rotary hook machines were a hallmark of the Standard Sewing Machine Company; and in fact I would describe their old logo as a wildly-spinning wheel with wings. The rotary hook design is noted for continuous and smooth circular movement of the stitch forming mechanism, and this is absolutely necessary to keep a lightweight machine from walking around. Keep in mind that the rotary hook spins around a horizontal axis. There are other types of stitch forming mechanisms that use back and forth motion. You can visualize how such designs can result in machine walk, especially in a truly lightweight sewing machine. This rotary hook makes two revolutions per stitch. *Featherweights* were often demonstrated to prospective buyers by setting the little green attachment box on its side, and balancing the machine on top of it. Then the machine would be run (unthreaded) at full speed to show how little vibration there was. This helped show the uniqueness of the *221*. *Singer*, however, immensely improved on the operator's access to the bobbin case. The Sewhandy was a top-loading design, and was rather awkward to load. In the *Featherweight*, the swinging bed extension allowed easy access to insert the bobbin case directly from that end of the machine.

The last significant improvement was made to the bobbin winder. On the *Sewhandy*, the winder was simply an extension of the main shaft in the machine head, and it was necessary to run the stitching mechanism to wind a bobbin. The Model *221* was designed so the balance wheel could be released through a simple stop motion screw, allowing the operator to wind bobbins without running the needle mechanism and its drive parts. *Singer* also added an adjustment feature to allow bobbins to be wound evenly. By loosening a single screw, its bobbin winder tensioner could be moved left-right to adjust how the thread was tracking on the bobbin. A final amenity was the addition of a thread cutter on its presser foot shaft.

The Product

To sum it up, the new *Featherweight* was quite a sewing machine! In its shiny black japan finish and fancy gold trim, it stood proudly in *Singer* stores and company salesmen's arms across the country. Its design improvements took it many giant steps ahead of the *Sewhandy*, which had set the stage, and apparently the sewing public agreed. *Singer* once advertised that it's "probably been put under more Christmas trees than any other portable electric in the world". Well put! To say that the *Featherweight Model 221* was a popular machine would be a gross understatement!

22

CHAPTER FIVE

PRODUCTION HISTORY

This chapter results from extensive study of over sixty *Featherweight* machines I have personally owned, plus the research notes I've taken on many more of them in quilting classes across the country. In addition, the *Singer Sewing Company* was especially helpful in providing technical assistance to my first book project, upon which this revised and updated version is based. And finally, I have loads of information gleaned from over seven hundred letters sent to me over the past four years by *Model 221* owners. Let me say that the production data in this book is significantly more accurate and complete than in my first edition. Why? Simply because I have a much larger technical data base on *Featherweights* than I did in 1992. The information contained here is as complete as it can be at this time, and I do not believe it will be substantially improved through future research.

I'll start with what will be a controversial statement. *Featherweights* were made in only three basic colors - black, beige, and white. The vast majority of the black machines have the shiny black japan finish, but some were apparently manufactured under government contract in a black crinkle. I've heard this alternate finish also called black matte. Note also that the beige color is often called tan. And the white-colored machines may be pearl white, or they may have very slight tints of green or brown (the brown-tinted version is called bisque). Needless to say there is a lot of inter-mixing of the beige, tan and bisque terminology. This adds to the confusion.

Yes, I know there are legends of red, dark green, light and dark blue, and dark brown machines. However, I have never personally seen any of these color variations. And I've never been able to get a photo of one of these elusive devils when responding to folks who claimed to own one. I'll write more about these legends in a later chapter.

The black-color japan finish machines are, by far, the most commonly seen. They were manufactured (the term "birthdated" will be introduced in a later chapter) over about a twenty eight year span between 1933 and 1961, although sales from warehouse and store stocks apparently lasted well beyond 1961. Some references show that manufacturing continued until 1964, but I haven't been able to confirm this with factory serial number records. Incidentally, the term "japan" refers to a hard, brilliant black finish that was used by *Singer*. It's always spelled japan, not Japan.

In my first *Featherweight* book I speculated that 221's were also made in Great Britain; and I've confirmed this as fact since then. I know now that *Featherweights* were manufactured in Great Britain from the late forties into the sixties, and were sold across the world. Many were imported into Canada, apparently being assembled with Canadian-made motors when they were landed. And some younger ones were sold in the States during the late fifties and early sixties, after production of the U.S. black-colored version was curtailed.

All of the imported British black-colored machines I have seen are equipped with motors marked: "*The Singer Mfg. Co.*, St. Johns, P.Q. . . . . , made in Canada". This label data has led to wide speculation that the <u>entire</u> machine was manufactured in St. Johns, Quebec, Canada - which I believe to be incorrect. A careful observer will see that many machines are marked "made in Great Britain" on the arm, even though their motors indicate "made in Canada". Why, you ask, were the basic machines built in Great Britain, and their motors in Canada? I don't have a definitive answer but I can speculate.

British household electric supply is nominally 230 volts A.C. (alternating current), and there were numerous other A.C. and D.C. (direct current) voltages in use elsewhere across the world. There still are! However, Canada and the U.S. had standardized their household supply at 110-120 volts A.C. So, machines intended for the Canadian and U.S. markets needed these motors; and it may be that the St. Johns factory was Singer's choice to source them. Why didn't the Clydebank factory simply supply motors of the proper voltage for Canada or the U.S.? It may be there was a tariff or even political considerations from importing complete, ready-to-go machines.

I often seen black-colored *Model 221's* for sale that have 230 -250 volt motors. It appears that these machines were originally sold in the U.K. and other countries where this higher voltage was (or is) the local line standard. Usually their new U.S. owners are trying to sell the machine after searching, unsuccessfully, for a factory original 110/120 volt motor. (The foot controller must also be changed, but they are more readily available.) These machines can present good value if the new owner is willing to have a currently made, non-original motor installed. The opposite scenario also occurs. A machine with a U.S. voltage motor is taken to the U.K., Europe or the Far East. However, in this case all that's required is a common traveler's voltage step-down transformer to plug the machine into.

Black-Colored Machines

The basic, black U.S. machine is the Model 221, made at the Elizabethport, New Jersey factory. The British-made black machine is the Model 221K. The letter K on all British machines indicates the Kilbowie factory. This factory, on the edge of Glasgow, Scotland, was at Clydebank - probably so named for being on the banks of the Clyde River. Some sources have incorrectly named this site as "Clydeside". Please note that a number suffix was also used to indicate model improvements over time, for example 221-1. The model variations seem to be 221-1, 221K1, 221K4, and 221K5 - although there are serious questions about the K5 ever having been made in black. The jury may still be out on this one. All U.S. and British black-colored machines have a gear driven shaft for the mechanism in their lower bed housing.

The first U.S. black-colored machines were indicated as model 221's without a dash or suffix number. Their reason for transition into 221-1's is not clear, probably lost in the mists of history. Many people have asked me about it. My judgment is that it coincided with the change to the "later style" rotary sewing hook in 1934-35. The "early style" used a different arm shaft, sewing hook and collar and counterbalance. Its bobbin case base could not be removed without taking the hook off the shaft and disassembling it - a major undertaking. The "later style" was more easily accessed, as you will learn later in this book.

Model 221 - Series AD (early)

The British made machines were introduced after the "later style" rotary sewing hook was standard, so the first machines were 221K's, actually it's the variation 221K1. A later variant was the 221K4 which used a different light cover and switch. The switch is a toggle type on the right end of the light socket. The series K4 machine also used a motor that was equipped with radio frequency suppressers and grounded wiring. Apparently this was a sign of the times. Next in line, the 221K5 machine reverted to a toggle switch in the same location on the bed as the early machines. There are some *Featherweight* collectors who insist that the 221K5 was only made in the color generally referred to as tan, and which Singer called both light bisque and beige (this is the 221J). Nonetheless, I believe that at least some japan black versions were made. I'll write about this later.

Model 221K4 Sewing Light

Featherweight Model 221K5

The K5 version used a pressed steel, painted face plate instead of the shiny plated earlier ones. The same type of face plate was later supplied with the 221K7. The 221K5 bobbin winder is also different, having a projection to make it easier to move in and out of the "wind" position. There is also a change in the stitch length lever and nut.

White-Colored Machines

The white-colored machine is the Model 221K7, also made at the Clydebank factory in Scotland. Again, let me say that this white machine may be pearl white, or it may have very slight tints of green or brown. *Singer* called the pearl white version <u>white</u>, and the tinted ones are named <u>bisque</u> and <u>green</u>, respectively. The bisque name is appropriate (cream is another term that I hear), but the green just doesn't seem to fit. Yes, a few of them are painted in a light green-color but most are very pale green. Their colors have a wide range within the light green band. In fact, I've had a suggestion that we *Featherweight* owners band together to re-name the lightest green color - "barely celery". That's what it is! This would avoid a lot of confusion and wasted effort by collectors searching for the rumored green (and I mean <u>green</u>) 221 machines that just don't exist! I've also heard of a blue-tinted version of the 221K7 and several men who serviced *Singer* machines have written that they've worked on them. But I've never seen one myself. And a search of an older *Singer* parts catalog only showed colored parts for the white, green and bisque versions of the Model 221K7.

Several references, including some sewing machine authorities, state that the 221K7 was made from 1968-70, and were sold in the U.S. during this same period. But I now believe this information is incorrect. I think it's a case of repeated quoting and repetition of the same sources. I have a letter in my files from a woman in Michigan who received a white-colored 221K7 at Christmas, 1965 - a present to be used in her Dorm room at the State University. She wrote that the instruction booklet is copyrighted 1964. Another woman wrote to me from Wisconsin, sending a copy of a sales receipt for $149.50 which was dated November of 1965. It's for a green-tinted 221K7 she bought on installments at a *Singer* store in Boise, Idaho. Still

others have written that they were available in the U.S. as early
as 1964. So, with this new data I will say that the white-colored
Featherweights were sold in the U.S. from about 1964 to 1970.
They were certainly made as early as 1964, as evidenced by
serial number records.

Featherweight Model 221K7

Mowry Photo

One of the significant differences of the 221K7 as
compared with the black and beige (tan) *Featherweights* is
that it has a shorter swinging bed extension. The K7 version
is only 3 1/2-inches long, as compared with 5 1/2-inches on the
regular *Model 221*. Also, it uses a timing belt linkage between
its arm and hook shafts, rather than an upright arm shaft and
gears. Distrust in this design, even by service and repair people,
may account in part for its lesser value today. But the timing
belt has held up pretty well, and it's been almost unanimously
adopted by modern sewing machine manufacturers. Also,
the motor controller on the 221K7 is more or less permanently

wired into the machine, as opposed to being removable by using a push/pull pin connector. Its light switch was changed to a rotary type, but still in the familiar location on the right top of the bed. The machine only has a painted finish, including its face plate, and it doesn't have the fancy gold trim decals as with the black-colored machines. Most of these changes were undoubtedly cost cutting measures.

There is one curiosity with the 221K7 machines. Apparently, some were marketed under different model numbers. This may have been an attempt to spruce up the fading image of the old *Model 221*. A woman in Ohio wrote that she bought what she thought was a *Featherweight*, but was told it was a 328K. She said it is white with a hint of green, and it came in a mint green case trimmed in white with one latch. On the right side it says "221K" in black. The serial number starts with EV and the Singer folks told her it was made [birthdated] on May 13, 1964. Comment by NJ-S: this machine is indeed a *Featherweight!*

Beige (Tan) Machines
This brings me to the more limited production beige-colored machine. It's often called tan but it has two factory color designations: "light bisque" and "beige". I've seen both in the literature but I avoid using <u>light bisque</u> because, as we've seen, the 221K7 color is called <u>bisque</u>. This can be very confusing, even to service and repair people, so I'll just use beige (tan) hereafter in this book.

Mechanically this machine is the 221K5, painted in *Singer's* beige, and labeled the Model 221J. To confuse things a bit more, there are also 221J6 models, and this specific model number is indicated on the little plate that's riveted to the lower part of the machine arm. The 221J and 221J6 models seem to be one-in-the-same machine design. Both of them are often mistaken for the bisque-colored 221K7, however the J-machines have the regular 5 1/2-inch long swinging bed extension, rather than the shorter K7 extension (3 1/2-inch). Incidentally, some of the 221J motor controllers are beige and others are somewhat darker - I would call this alternate color light brownish mustard. I don't know why the two colors were used.

It's widely believed that all model 221J machines were manufactured at the St. Johns factory in Quebec, Canada. This is debatable. The machines I've owned and seen, and those that have been reported to me, all have serial numbers that begin with an ES or ET, or a JE prefix. (One exceptional 221J machine I know of is owned by a woman in California. It has serial number E159456 - the E doesn't have a suffix nor a prefix - and she's even dusted with a white powder to look for it.)

So why do some of these comparatively rare 221J's have ES and ET prefixes and others have the JE prefix? ES and ET prefixes were used by Clydebank in Scotland. I suspect these 221J machines were actually British-made 221K5's painted in the beige color. Others, perhaps a very few, were finished in japan black. Moving to the JE prefix machines, they may have been manufactured from scratch at St. Johns; or they could have been produced at Clydebank and imported into Canada where they were painted beige and supplied with their motors and motor controllers. Both parts are certainly marked "St. Johns, P.Q.", but as yet there is no hard evidence that the <u>entire</u> machine was manufactured in Canada. There is one hint, though. The serial number on all JE prefix machines I've personally seen was <u>stamped upside down</u> from the usual position on all other Featherweight models. That is, the figures can be read when the bed extension is facing downward, rather than when the handwheel is down. This suggests a different production process or convention. With this in mind I believe that the 221J's with ES and ET serial number prefixes are British-made at Clydebank, originally indicated as 221K5 machines in beige color.

Model 221J Identification Plate

31

And those with the JE prefix were produced or at least assembled at St. Johns, Quebec. The latter may be marked 221J6 or 221J. Some limited data suggests that the J6 marking is the earlier version.

I own an absolutely original JE prefix machine with serial number JE 156107. The machine is marked 221J. It came with an instruction booklet that's marked 221K5 and "printed in Great Britain". I've never seen nor heard of an instruction booklet marked 221J or 221J6. Apparently, all of the machines were supplied with this same 221K5 booklet.

Ample birthdate data indicates these beige machines were made and marketed in the early nineteen-sixties, from 1960 into 1962, but this date range may be expanded with further research. Also, more data is needed to positively fix the 221J manufacturing sites or site. All 221J's are gear driven, same design as the black-colored 221 and 221K Model variations. However, no gold trim bed decals were used as with the regular black 221's and the 222K.

The End, Or Was It?
With this production history behind us you may wonder why the *Featherweight* was discontinued? With increased research and many letters from older owners and retired service and repair men, I've firmed up what was a tentative conclusion in the first edition of this book. Simply, the *Featherweight* fell to an unfortunate combination of increased production costs and falling consumer demand. Most everyone over the age of forty or so has seen the rapid rise in the cost of quality goods in the stores. Considering that manufacturers are in business to make a profit for their owners and stockholders, increases in the cost to produce a product must be offset somehow, or passed along to the consumer. And so it was (and is) with sewing machines. Apparently the *Featherweight* had become an expensive machine to produce, and its retail pricing reflected this fact. It was designed back in the nineteen thirties with the labor intensive manufacturing technology of that era. By the sixties it was competing with less expensive machines that were built using more modern, automated technology.

The falling demand part of the scene was that the *Featherweight* just didn't offer what most sewing machine buyers were looking for back in the nineteen fifties and sixties. By the start of the fifties decade American women were ready for zigzag machines. Two companies started to import them by the late forties; import tariffs were low to help rebuild Europe after World War Two. Zigzag machines became extremely popular, changing women's fashion and the sewing practices of most all home seamstresses. Hand sewing was virtually eliminated because these advanced machines could do most everything by moving a lever or pushing a button. And imported zigzags were priced about the same as U.S. made straight stitch machines. These new-wave machines created a rebirth of home sewing.

Both points were driven home to me in a letter from a former *Singer* salesman. He related how he started working for the company in 1967 and found that he couldn't give a [black] 221 away. He also wrote that he took over a shop in Vermont and went down the cellar, seeing it was full of them [221's] - about 25-30! He said the new white one was selling for $129.95, but was always on sale for $99.00, so you could not sell the black ones for $59.00. His last comment was . . . . he should have bought all of them himself at $59.00. Readers can add an exclamation point to that last sentence!

By the time the sixties came, the *Featherweight* portable sewing machine was an anachronism, an expensive machine to manufacture, not unlike many other products that were designed decades before. And it didn't offer the same desirable features as did its competition. So production of the basic black *Model 221* was phased out at Clydebank in about 1962. Factory warehouse and store stocks undoubtedly lasted for some months or years to come, as evidenced by many correspondents who report buying brand new black-colored Featherweights after that year. Many of these are 221K's that are marked "Made in Great Britain" on the machine arm or bed. Its replacement on the portable sewing machine stage was the white-colored Model 221K7, also imported from Great Britain. Apparently its manufacturing costs were lower. But it was the last gasp for the *Featherweight*. The machine just didn't offer the features that most women wanted at the time. It only lasted in the U.S. market until about 1970.

Tides will flow, and then they ebb. But the *Featherweight* odyssey continued. I'll say the *Model 221* was only biding its time. It refused to die. And it emerged only two decades later as perhaps the preeminent portable sewing machine in a quilt making world dominated by computer controlled wonders. How did this happen? Simple! The old *Featherweight* is perfectly suited for modern quilt making and their makers, and in this regard it's achieved status as a true classic. The tide is back!

CHAPTER SIX

BIRTHDATES!

Many *Featherweight* owners think affectionately of their machine and the date it was made, referring to the latter as its "birthdate". The word has come into common use with respect to *Model 221's* over the past four years, and I've heard it from quilters, machine owners and collectors. I'm told there's *Featherweight* activity on the Internet - with a lot of e-mail referencing birthdates. I've even heard of 221 machines with the same birthdate being referred to by their owners as "twins". Overall, I like this birthdate concept because it reflects the affection and prestige of owners in their machine, its history, and the women (or men) it may have served over the years. To many people their *Model 221* is more than just a sewing machine; it's more of a personal link to the past and times and places that will never be forgotten.

On the subject of birthdates, let me say that I <u>do not</u> believe that *Singer* kept records of the exact date when every single machine left the production line or factory. So, the word "birthdate" may be a bit misleading. Yes, I know these are controversial statements. However, I've carefully studied serial number records and have seen that many, many *Featherweight* machines apparently left the factory on a single day. In some cases almost 20,000 machines have the same reported birthdate! This production rate for sewing machines like *Model 221's* is highly unlikely even with a huge factory like the Elizabethport site. Now, punching out 20,000 throat plates in one day, no problem. 20,000 rotary hook assemblies, maybe. But 20,000 *Featherweights* in a single day - I'd have to see it to believe!

So how can this be? A probable explanation is that the so-called birthdate is the date when a block or lot of serial numbers was assigned to the sewing machine model that was being produced at that time. This means that the birthdate <u>is not</u> the exact date of production of a specific machine. Instead, it would be the date when the production process began for a particular run or lot of Featherweights.

Owners have asked me to birthdate their machine. It isn't possible to determine the exact date without referring to *Singer* factory records; and from what I've heard they've been overloaded with requests. Most people don't need an exact date anyway; the year of manufacture is close enough. To help with this I produced a table in the original edition of this book that allowed folks to find their machine's year with good accuracy. I've been able to improve this table over the past four years because a much larger database of serial numbers is now available to me. Also, I'm now able to share production history on the black-colored British 221K machines, and on the 222K Free Arm *Featherweight Convertibles*. Serial number information was virtually non-existent on both machines when I first wrote about them four years ago. Finally, I've included manufacturing year information for the white or white-tinted British 221K7 machines, and for the beige (tan) 221J model variant.

An important fact to keep in mind is that there <u>was not</u> a separate or special serial number series just for *Featherweights*. This has confused many people and it makes birthdating a bit more complicated. I believe *Singer* chose to assign machine serial numbers to specific models in small blocks or lots as the machines were scheduled for production, or possibly during the assembly process. Most likely this happened with *Featherweights* when their beds were being machined. For example, a *Model 221* machine with serial number AF 123456 might be one of 10,000 *Featherweights* that were assigned the block or lot from AF 120000 to AF 129999. Then, at serial number AF 130000 the next block or lot of numbers could have been assigned to another sewing machine model, for example, *Singer's* Model 201 machine.

To date your Model 221 machine you should turn it over to find the serial number that's stamped into its aluminum bed casting. If you have the regular black-colored U.S. made machine, the serial number will start with the letter A. Following the A is another letter which I named the "series number". These are the letters you need to determine the birthdate of your U.S. made Featherweight. Similarly, if you own the British 221K or the 222K Free Arm Featherweight Convertible, you will find the letter E, or possibly a F or a J, followed by another letter - again this is the series number. Refer to the appropriate table that follows in this section. There are also six digits which follow the two letters, examples: (U.S.) AF 123456, or (G.B.) EK 123456. These numbers are not necessary to allow you to "year date" your machine, though you can calculate closely to the month or months of its birthdate by a simple math proportion.

Model 221 U.S.

Model 221 British - Centennial

Model 221K7 Great Britian

Model 221J (serial no. upside down)

Model 222K Free Arm

Be careful of taking month calculations too far! Remember that the serial numbers for *Model 221's* (and other machines) were assigned in blocks. There could have been, and probably , periods of weeks or months before Model 221's were being run again on the production line. Statistically, *Featherweights* will not be evenly distributed across the entire serial number range. To quote my husband, Frank: "*Featherweight* collectors shouldn't try to hang out with mathematicians".

Legend:
E = early (Jan-April)
M = mid (May-Aug)
L = late (Sept-Dec)

TABLE 1
MODEL 221 (U.S)

Series Letter	Start - End
AD	E 1930 - L 1935
AE	L 1935 - M1938
AF	M1938 - M1941
AG	M1941 - E 1947
AH	E 1947 - L 1948
AJ	L 1948 - L 1950
AK	L 1950 - M 1952
AL	M1952 - E 1955
AM	E 1955 - E 1959
AN	E 1959

TABLE 2
MODELS 221K and 222K (Great Britain)

Series Letter	Start - End
ED	1941 - E 1947
EE	E 1947 - E 1949
EF	E 1949 - M1950
EG	M1950 - L 1951
EH	L 1951 - M1953
EJ	M1953 - L 1954
EK	L 1954 - L 1955
EL	L 1955 - L 1956
EM	L 1956 - L 1957
EN	L 1957 - E 1959
EP	E 1959 - E 1960
ER	E 1960 - L 1960
ES	L 1960 - L 1961
ET	L 1961 - E 1963
EV	E 1963 - M1964
EW	1968
EY	unknown, possibly 1969
FA	unknown, possibly 1970
JE	(St. Johns, P.Q. - 221J/J6) 1960 - 1961

Readers should keep in mind that the information in the preceding tables shows an <u>approximate</u> date of manufacture of your Featherweight sewing machine. Some machines were in warehouse or retail storage for months, or even years, before being sold to a consumer. Therefore, purchase date will always be later than manufacturing date.

How Many?

The question I'm asked most is . . . . how many *Featherweights* were made? I've speculated quite a bit on this and I know others have too. The machines were made since 1933 and were sold for some 37 years. After studying serial number records (which admittedly continue to evolve), and discounting the World War Two years when Singer was involved in essential wartime production, I've calculated to what I'll call an "educated guess". The total production of these wonderful sewing machines was probably between 3 and 3-1/2 million! One of my correspondents, a former shop owner in California, put it well. He wrote that the *Featherweight* was the best selling sewing machine ever built anywhere. Frankly, I believe it!

CHAPTER SEVEN

OTHER MANUFACTURING CHANGES

If you own several *Featherweights*, particularly the regular black-colored model, you'll probably see some more or less obvious changes in the design of the machine, and in the parts used in it. Some of these changes were made to improve its function, others helped it adapt to the customers and the market. Advancing technology allowed component parts to be made more simply or at a faster rate. Still other changes were cost cutting measures.

Face Plate

A good example of design changes is the face plate used on the 221, 221K and 222K machines. The early U.S. machines, beginning with series AD in 1933, have a fancy, decorative design on their face plates. I've heard it called "Egyptian Scrollwork" and it's really nice looking. Incidentally, there are two slightly different versions of this scrollwork design, and it takes a keen eye to discern the difference. In both examples, the scrollwork itself appears to have been punched into each individual face plate, using heavy machinery and a die to impress the design. A friend who's familiar with metal working tells me that the metal plate may have been heated while the punching process took place. Afterwards, the face plate was electroplated with its shiny surface coating, probably nickel or chromium, or both. Needless to say, this was a labor and energy intensive manufacturing process.

You may wonder, as I did, why *Singer* had two different scrollwork designs. The first one, without "wrap around" coverage in the area of the machine's take up lever and thread guide, was used up until about mid-1937 in series AE. Then the second version, with increased scrollwork coverage in the areas mentioned, began to be seen sporadically. Within a year or so, all machines had the second type - apparently as factory inventories of the first one were exhausted. My theory on why this happened is that the 221 machine just looked better from the operator's sewing position with the second type, so this improvement was incorporated into the punching dies as worn ones were being replaced.

Egyptian Scrollwork

Straited Face Plate

Later on, in early 1947 at about the start of the series AH, a newer design face plate began to be randomly seen. This design consists of vertical grooves or stripes that cover the entire surface of the plate. In the first edition of the book I coined the term "striated" for this design and I'm elated to hear and see that it's caught on with *Featherweight* enthusiasts. One year later, by about the mid-point of the AH series, all U.S. 221 machines were being supplied with this striated design. Why the change? I believe it was a cost cutting measure. A close examination of a striated plate shows that the grooves were not punched in place on individual units. Manufacturing technology had advanced such that metal could be purchased from mill suppliers in sheets, with grooves already formed in its surface. It was a simple matter of cutting and forming the metal to the size and contour needed for the face plate. And it didn't have to be heated while being formed. This change simplified the manufacturing process and thereby reduced costs.

The early British 221K machines were supplied with a mix of the two scrollwork designs, although the second type seems to be in the great majority. Then, at about the start of series EG in mid-1950, the striated design face plate began to be seen. Changeover appears to have been completed later in that series. Lastly, let me say that this striated face plate design was supplied with all of the 222K *Featherweight Convertible* machines.

The younger 221K5 and 221J beige machines, and the 221K7 white (or white tint) machines, were all supplied with a simple, pressed steel face plate. This plate does not have an impressed design and it's painted to match the machine. This is an extremely cost effective method of manufacturing the part. It represents the final stage of evolution of the *Featherweight* face plate.

Painted Face Plate (white)

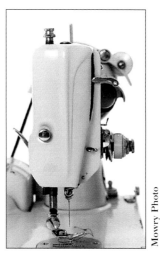

Painted Face Plate (beige)

Gold Trim Decal

Another readily apparent design change is to the gold trim decals on the machine bed and handwheel housing of the black-colored machines. *Singer's* official name for the decals is <u>transfers</u>, but most people call them decals so I'll use the term here to avoid confusion. There are two decal designs. The earlier one was used up to (about) the middle of series AL in the later part of 1953. On the British machines it went to (about) the start of the EJ series in late 1954. It's hard to describe the design with words so please refer to the photo reference here. My best stab is it looks like the decal connects every couple of inches with intertwined arms. Most people, including me, refer to this gold decal design as the early one.

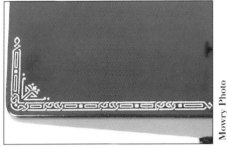

Early Decal Design

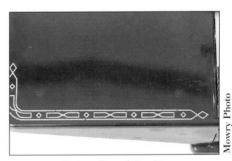

Prism Decal Design

The later type of gold trim decal is not as pretty, in my opinion. I call it the "Prism Design". It consists of rectangle and diamond shapes, with grossly elongated X's that are made from two of the shapes that quilters call a prism. The point of each prism touches the adjoining one; and the X repeats about every 1-1/2 inch in the main bed decal. In reviewing serial number data, it seems that both the U.S and British factories both changed over to the Prism Design very quickly. Dates were mentioned earlier. There was not a lengthy transition period when both types of decals were used. Apparently inventory of the earlier type was not large at either factory site.

Why the change to the gold trim decals? Simply, I don't really know for sure. And I haven't been able to get a definitive answer from correspondents who were former Singer factory and sales personnel. I suspect it was made to help modernize the appearance of the *Featherweight*. The change was made in the early nineteen fifties, after the basic 221 was around for about twenty years. Admittedly, the early type design looks a bit "antiquey". Similar designs had been used by Singer on other machine models since the turn of the century. It may be that the Prism Design decal was an attempt to help bring the machine into the post war era. Looking backwards, it may have been a prophesy - since *Featherweights* are in such high demand today by quilters!

Bobbin Winder Tensioner

The very earliest U.S. made *Featherweights* have a bobbin winder tension bracket on the right <u>front</u> of the machine bed. This tensioner was designed to keep the thread taut when a bobbin was being wound. Also, by loosening a single screw, the bracket and its spring-loaded tension wheels could be moved left-right to adjust how the thread was tracking on the bobbin. The front bed location was phased out in the 1936-38 time frame, probably during machine Series AE. I'm going to say that this change coincided with the introduction of the Model 308 Folding Utility Table (Card Table). Why? Simply because the tensioner's front bed location would require a special cut-out in an otherwise straight edge in the Card Table opening. And even with a cut-out, it would be difficult to thread the tension wheels on its front bracket. So, the bobbin winder tensioner was moved to its more familiar location on the right top of the machine bed. This made for a more streamlined machine - a better candidate for something like a Card Table - and easier to use when it was in the Table.

This later style tensioner functions the same and just as well as the earlier version. It's used on all 221-1, 221K1, 221K4, 221K5 and 222K Free Arm machines. A simpler version, without tension wheels but still with left-right adjustment, is used on the British 221K7 "white" *Featherweight*.

Mowry Photo

Model 221K7 Bobbin Winder Tensioner

Seam Allowance Gauge

Early machines had a plain chromed throat plate, without markings for seam allowances. However, the newer machines were supplied with a seam allowance gauge that was stamped into the machine's throat plate, and this feature is readily visible. There are two types. One type has the seam allowance marked in 1/8-inch increments, from 1/8-inch up to 3/4-inch. And the second type of plate, which seems to be more common, is marked with numbers from 2 through 8. Each number and its corresponding line represents a 1/8-inch increment from the center line of the needle. Therefore, using line 2 as an edge guide, the seamstress would get a 1/4-inch seam allowance; line 5 would be 5/8-inch; etc. Gauge-type throat plates began to be seen on U.S. machines at about the start of series AL in mid 1952. It also appeared at the start of series EJ, in late 1954, on British 221K machines. I suspect there was some retrofitting of face plates, by owners, both ways. In some cases, a woman might install a gauge-type throat plate on an early machine. The opposite also occurred, i.e., a plain throat plate was installed on a younger machine that was originally supplied with the seam allowance version. Both types were readily available from Singer parts stock.

Stamped Throat Plate

A different throat plate was supplied on all 222K Free Arm machines. This plate is longer than the basic 221 plate. It's stamped with fractional markings and lines, rather than numbers and lines. Again, the fractions start at 1/4-inch and go up to 3/4-inch, in 1/8-inch increments - representing the range of all commonly used seam allowances. I have never seen a 222K machine that did not have this gauge-type throat plate.

Model 222K Throat Plate

Needle Tension Adjustment

There were more subtle changes. The first U.S. black-colored *Model 221's* without a dash or suffix number were the ones with the early style needle tension adjustment. Up until (about) the middle of series AF (mid 1940), this tension adjustment was a simple thumb nut to adjust spring pressure on the tension discs. It didn't have index markings to allow the user to repeat a particular setting, so adjusting needle tension was a bit time consuming when sewing on different fabrics. An improvement was made to the later machines by redesigning to include a numbered dial. The British made machines were changed over to the numbered dial tension adjustment during series EH in 1952.

Electrical Parts

If your *Featherweight* is in factory-supplied condition (many are not) and it has a toggle type on-off switch on the right end of the light socket, it's a Model 221K4. This light socket type switch is a feature the 221K4 shared with most, if not all, of the 222K Free Arm machines. All other 221, 221K and 221J machines had their light switches in a raised boss on the bed just to the right of the machine arm. The series K4 machine also used a motor that was equipped with radio frequency suppressers and grounded wiring. If it's original to the machine, its motor will be marked CAK7, possibly with a dash and number following it. This motor improvement was made in the early 1950's to reduce static interference after home television sets became more common.

I've found that sewing machine collectors, in particular, take pains to insure that their machines are "right" with respect to being factory original. That is, all parts should be original to the machine or at least to the time period. Generally, with *Featherweights* it's the motor or motor controller that fails first. Owners also changed motors when moving to/from countries with different household line voltages. Although brand new factory motors are not available today, they were in the past; and many machines were fitted with replacements that are not original to the machine. For those who are interested in these details, I've prepared a chart listing the factory specification motors for all of the 221 machine model variations.

Model	Motor
221	3-110
221-1	3-110 or 3-120
221K4	CAK7
221K5 and 221J's	CAJ6
221K7	CAK8
222K	CAJ6 or CAK7

Series 3 motors were built in the U.S. before February, 1954. The dash following the basic number 3 shown in the table indicates the maximum voltage the motor was designed for. Examples: 3-32 indicates 32 volts (which would be D.C), and 3-110 indicates 100-110 volts (A.C or D.C). British motors will be marked 3-220, 3-230, or 3-250 - as they were supplied for the higher household line supply there. This convention applies to A.C. voltages at the most common range of 25-75 cycles per second (c.p.s.). A slightly different one was used for 80-100 c.p.s.

CA series motors were supplied after February, 1954 . A different numbering system was used for them.

-1	12 volts D.C.
-3	32 volts D.C.
-5	50 volts AC/DC
-6	95-100 volts AC/DC
-7	100-110 volts AC/DC
-8	110-120 volts AC/DC
-9	150-165 volts AC/DC
-10	190-210 volts AC/DC
-11	210-230 volts AC/DC
-12	230-250 volts AC/DC
-14	120-130 volts AC/DC
-15	130-145 volts AC/DC

Some readers may think this is academic information; let me share how it played out in practice. The *Featherweight* was distributed and used in the far reaches of the world, and the smorgasbord of special motors was available and used. One woman from Africa wrote that she did missionary work in Tanzania for many years. Though there was no electricity at the mission, she did use her *Featherweight* to make and repair clothes. The machine had what she said was a "special motor", and she could only sew when an occasional safari party arrived in the village. Her 221 would be wired up to several Land Rover and truck batteries in series and she would happily sew all night while the visitors slept!

Other Changes

The last minor changes I'll mention were to the bobbin winder, and the stitch length lever and its lock nut. The bobbin winder on the 221K5 and 221J6 machines has a projection or lug to make it easier to move in and out of the "wind" position. It increases the leverage of the operator's fingers. This is a good example of a functional improvement; although it did not carry over to the later 221K7 British version of the *Featherweight*.

Model 221K5 Bobbin Winder

Flat Stitch Length Lever

Stitch Length Lever - later plastic type

A change was also made on the K5, J6 and K7 machines, eliminating the flat thumb piece on the end of the stitch length lever. It was changed to a simple machine screw design, and a captive plastic knob was added to be used to lock in position. This was undoubtedly a cost cutting change.

Finally, let me say that there were other, less significant, production changes over the years. I will not attempt to list or comment on these as they are of technical importance only to advanced collectors. So they are outside the scope of this chapter and book.

CHAPTER EIGHT

FINDING A FEATHERWEIGHT

Back in 1989, three years before writing the first edition of this book, I didn't own even one *Featherweight* machine. And since then I've bought upwards of sixty of the critters. I've sold or given away most of them to relatives. But I've kept a few myself. I've also helped some friends find a machine or two for their own use. What started out as a search for just one machine had me sleuthing for another one or two, then it cascaded into a research project for my book. A correspondent wrote that they're like potato chips, you have one and you want more and more.

While traveling on the quilt teaching circuit I've seen literally thousands of *Featherweights* in classes and seminars across the country. My "educated guess" is that 3 to 3-1/2 million of these fine machines were made (see Chapter 6). Most are still out there and some few are for sale. Just how do you find one?

My Search for a *Featherweight*

Although it's a classic, I would hardly call the *Singer Featherweight* an antique, but that's where I started out to find one - the antique shops. I can laugh about some of my experiences today, but they didn't seem quite as funny at the time. Usually my inquiry about old sewing machines resulted in an escort to a side aisle or corner where an early treadle machine reposed along with stacks of musty old newspapers and magazines. Or possibly it was an early cast iron portable was offered, well encased in its round-top wooden cover. "No, no - you don't understand! I'm looking for a small portable *Singer* machine in a small black case. They were made up into the sixties". The typical response to this plea was a short lecture on how the proprietor only dealt in true antiques. Really old machines! One antique shop owner told me to come back in about twenty years. But once in a while I came across a shop owner who knew what I was looking for. Invariably, though, I heard how I should have come in last week or last month, or maybe how there was one that went for all of twenty dollars last Fall at a local estate sale. Although I left many business cards for people to call me if they found one, I never received a single return call from any of these contacts. I started thinking about those mythical gremlins and their mischief; maybe one or two were working against me!

Asking in quilting and sewing shops did no better. Here, at least, the owners knew exactly what I wanted, but I usually faced a long waiting list, with no guarantee I'd ever receive a call. "They're very hard to find" sums up many conversations quite well.

Then, in 1990, I was teaching at the American International Quilt Association (AIQA) Festival in Houston, Texas. I saw several black-colored *Model 221's* that were for sale in the three hundred dollar range. Now three hundred dollars is no small amount - then as well as now - but I was getting desperate. I wanted a *Featherweight* and I was tired of running into dead ends. I rationalized that the price was actually a bargain considering what I'd heard *Model 221's* sold for when new, and the depreciated dollars I would be using in 1990. Unfortunately, I was busy with classes throughout the Festival and when I went back later with cash in hand, all the machines were gone. They'd literally slipped through my fingers. To say I was disappointed would be putting it rather mildly. Let's just say it was somewhere between disappointed and berserk!

When I got back home, I "took the bull by the horns". I told my husband I wanted to see a *Featherweight* under the Christmas tree. I knew if anyone could find one, Frank would. And I started reading the Household Appliance ads in the classified section of our newspapers. We get weekly and biweekly publications in the mail that list all kinds of goodies for sale, and I eagerly scanned them too.

I discovered that folks rarely advertised a *Featherweight* or a *Model 221* machine (even today it isn't the norm). Usually they're loosely described with something like: "Singer sewing machine, or Singer portable". You have to call to find out if it might be a

Featherweight. Most of them aren't so don't be disappointed. And even when it does sound like a *Featherweight* you can still strike out after arriving at the seller's home with pounding heart and cash in your wallet.

I'll never forget one *"Featherweight"* I found. I saw a *Singer* portable sewing machine advertised in our local paper. I called the number and spoke with a man who answered all of my questions correctly. Yes, the machine was black, it had a small drop-down table on its left, a shiny face plate with lines that ran up and down (striated) and a small black carrying case. And, yes, it was very light weight - only about ten pounds. Well, it sure sounded like a *Featherweight* and, best of all, he only wanted five dollars for it because he didn't sew and had to move later that day. It was already afternoon and the location was about 3 or 4 miles away from where my husband works. I called him to stop on the way home. Then I waited patiently, and I must say, very happily. I was pleased with my work. Frank came home . . . . NO! NO! I guess the gremlins' work that day was to make me humble. It turned out to be a Model 319W *Singer* machine, no swinging bed extension, with a black painted face plate and a white-color carrying case. As I write this it sits in the corner of our garage, all 26 pounds in its case. Frank recognized it wasn't a *Featherweight* after arriving at the seller's home, but he bought it anyway because the foot controller and thread tensioner parts looked like the ones on a Model 221. He was thinking spare parts. It was definitely worth the five dollars, but it wasn't a Featherweight!

But we started finding them! Santa Claus surprised me with not one, but two machines under the Christmas tree! I just knew Santa could do it! One day I bought two *Featherweights* within a mile of each other. One of them was used almost daily by its original owner, and the other hadn't been used in about twenty years and was stored in the machine shed out back of a barn. Its owner knew she had it somewhere and we searched for about an hour before locating it. I found another one proudly standing as a bookshelf end - holding a long and somewhat precarious collection of hard covers. It hadn't ever been used by its owner. We replaced it with a couple of bricks before I left. Frank surprised me another time when I returned home after a long teaching job. I was greeted by a *Featherweight* and its Card Table standing in our living room. And I bought another one, on speculation, that had been almost completely disassembled for some reason. It came complete with a cardboard box full of small parts. Frank put it back together and found it was missing only its bobbin case. Fortunately I had an extra one that came with another machine. We have no idea why it was ever taken apart. Oh, if only these machines could talk!

Let me relate a typical success story. A woman in New Zealand wrote about the 222K Free Arm machine she found at a local weekly auction. She and her husband . . . . "spotted the familiar case of the 221. I opened the lid to check and found the machine to be a 222K. I couldn't believe my eyes but I just couldn't allow myself to be excited because one of the auction staff was nearby and he might think it rare and valuable and the bidding would start high. I re read the bit in your book about the 222K and as you mentioned you had only seen one in Canada at the time of writing the book. Fortunately, the story has a happy ending. My husband went to the auction and now we are the happy owners of a 222K".

And so it goes. You'll find them by searching the ads and markets in your hometown, or the next town or two away. Consider placing an advertisement yourself. Along this line, I'm told that folks are buying and selling *Featherweights* through the Internet. Quilting shops and quilt guilds are always a good potential source of machines, as are the vendor rows at larger quilt shows. *Featherweights* are not particularly scarce; it's just a matter of deciding you want one and investing the time and effort to find a machine that's for sale. Besides the common 221 variants, you may be rewarded with a very early machine, a scarcer version like the 221J beige-color machine or even a 222K Free Arm. And running into one of the limited editions that are described in a later chapter is always a possibility.

Pricing

How about pricing? In the brief years since the first edition of this book was published I've seen *Featherweight* prices continue to escalate. Large numbers of individuals and dealers consider the purchase of a *Model 221* a sound investment. In fact, in recent years in the U.S. the machines have appreciated at rates far exceeding inflation in the general economy. Friends in the U.K. tell me that recognition and demand (and prices) are sharply rising there as well, and to a similar extent in Canada. And prices are starting to track upwards from reports of correspondents in Australia, Mexico, New Zealand, South America and South Africa. This reflects the loyalty and great interest in the machine by large numbers of people - both were well earned by years of solid performance and renewed consumer demand. Another factor is that more and more people are getting to know about the *Singer Featherweight 221* machine through publications and word of mouth.

The increase in *Featherweight* recognition abroad is shown through a letter I received in 1994 from a woman in New Zealand. She wrote that she had contact with an embroidery/patchwork tutor years before, and the tutor. . . . "told us about these wonderful machines [Featherweights] she had seen while in America. At that time I don't think that she had found one here. In 1991 I saw one in the window of our local Singer centre, and asked if it was for sale. The owner said it wasn't, but after a lot of persuasion he changed his mind. It cost $500. (NZ) - about $250. (US). I thought it was quite expensive considering that my new computerised machine only cost $1500. (NZ), but it [the Featherweight] was certainly worth it . . . . It is really wonderful, and a joy to use . . . . It does a really great job of machine quilting".

I think we'll continue to see a slight upward pricing trend for *Model 221's*. Demand certainly isn't declining or even leveling off. Actually, I'm talking to more and more people who are looking for them. At present, a good used black *Model 221* will sell for $300. to $500. in the U.S., and excellent to mint original machines command much higher values. Although purists prefer the gear drive of the black-color machines, the value of the 221K7 "white" version is not far behind. Yes, I still hear about the $20. finds at local garage and yard sales, but they are becoming very much fewer and far between. Almost everyone who sews has heard about the *Featherweight*.

Values of the less-common variants like the beige-color 221J/J6 seem to be escalating at a higher rate. Likewise for the 222K Free Arm machines. I know of *Featherweight Convertible* Free Arms that were sold recently in the $1500. to $2000. range. Also, as knowledge of the scarcer editions (Exposition models, Blackside machines and others I'll write about later) is increasing, so too are their prices. For example, while at the AIQA Quilt Festival in Houston last year (1996) I learned of a black crinkle Finish machine that was purchased for $1200. Summing up, my prediction is that values for all unusual variations will rise dramatically over the next few years. Simply because more examples come to light, and collectors will acknowledge they exist and how rare they really are. Also, I believe that the 222K Free Arms, in particular, are poised to "go through the roof". I'll write about these in the next chapter.

Some collectors are stockpiling *Featherweights*, and others aren't. One man I know on the west coast had one hundred plus machines at last count and he isn't selling any. In fact, he stores his in some vault-like containers. Another man from Louisiana wrote that he's in the sewing machine business and has been selling and repairing for many years. In 1993 he said he had fourteen to keep as an investment. Then again, a good friend in the southwest who buys and sells *Featherweights* told me he turned over about seventy machines just last year. All told, I'd rather see these wonderful sewing machines out sewing. The *Featherweight* is almost like a race car, it's designed to go and it's all business - it just begs to be touched, handled and used.

A friends' Rose Garden and 34 Featherweights

Tom Martin and Marjorie McBride

The Future

The demand for these wonderful sewing machines will undoubtedly continue to increase. As my husband often says, "they're not making them any more". Yes, some very good portables are being manufactured, but they just aren't the same as the *Featherweight*. Unfortunately, our modern trends in manufacturing are away from simplicity and rugged construction, and toward the use of complex components, plastics and throw-aways. Against all this the *Featherweight* stands out as a benchmark. The Perfect Portable is a practical and steady performer in today's fast moving world. And at the same time it's a solid reminder of a simpler time era and its legacy in women's' sewing and quilt art.

CHAPTER NINE

FREE ARMS & GREMLINS

You've probably heard of the legend about gremlins, those creatures that humans blame for all sorts of things that don't go the way they should. Indeed, you wouldn't think a pleasant hobby such as researching and writing about *Featherweight* sewing machines would get much attention from these little creatures and the mischief they cause, but I believe it can! At least that's what a friend said when I told her about my troubles trying to find examples of the "Free Arm" *Featherweight* machine. She put me on to the gremlins. I thought they were involved early-on when I started looking for regular *Model 221's*. But when I began my search for a *Model 222K* Free Arm machine, it seemed as if an entire troop of gremlins decided to work against me, making things as difficult and frustrating as possible.

Mowry Photo

Singer® Model 222K Featherweight Convertible

That's how it's been for me and the intriguing - and elusive - *Singer Featherweight Convertible Model 222K*. It's commonly called the Free Arm machine because it has a tubular bed feature that allows stitching on curved or cylindrical articles of clothing, such as sleeves and pant legs, which would be inconvenient or impossible to handle on a flat bed plate machine. Almost from the moment I became interested in Featherweights, in the late 1980's, I wanted to get my hands on a 222K, own one, study it, compare parts, sew with it - do all the things that make research fun and rewarding. But the gremlins apparently decided it wasn't to be if they had anything to do with it. And the little fellows won out for well over six years! Why did it matter to me? Well, I already knew that the *Convertible 222K* was an especially rare *Featherweight* model, and that collector interest seemed really high. Well, it wasn't that I was being eccentric, possessive, or overly interested in their investment value. I literally needed one machine, two, or possibly more of them for essential research on this book.

But in nearly seven years of trying, I'd never had the chance to get my hands on a *222K Convertible*, nor had I found anyone with any good technical information on them. The gremlins were really working against me. Oh yes, I'd seen some 222K's in class, on occasion, during my quilt teaching travels. But it was always the same: it's not for sale! The best I could do was to look at the machines while teaching. And since I'm very busy during class I got precious little time to look. Also, some "hot leads" I had on available machines came to naught. Honestly, that's really an understatement. Blank, zero, zip - would be better! Yes, I did find some of them. One person wanted a queen's ransom for a Free Arm that was in absolutely deplorable condition. It looked as though it had fallen from a car that was moving at a pretty fast clip. Other so-called "Free Arms" turned out to be regular *Model 221's*. My husband made one memorable car trip of about 200 miles only to discover the machine wasn't the *Convertible 222K* its owner insisted it was over the course of several prior phone calls. We still don't understand how he confused the swinging flat bed extension on a regular *Model 221* with a removable extension plate and rounded bed. Still others I heard about across the country were already sold to buyers who had absolutely no intention of parting with their newly-found gem. One woman offered to loan a machine to me for research, but she was afraid to ship it for fear of damage or loss in transit. I just couldn't justify traveling to the West Coast to pick it up, and returning it in person later. My husband and I joked about traveling with the 222K chained to my wrist, like government couriers do with secret documents in an attaché case.

I finally got on the scoreboard thanks to two very dear friends, Floyd Turley of Oklahoma, and Marguerite Newell of Nova Scotia, Canada. Through their efforts, I came to own not one, but three Free Arms! Also - by pure coincidence, or possibly fate, I started receiving a lot of good information on 222K's from informed correspondents. Maybe someone had finally distracted those nasty gremlins!

I found that the *Featherweight Convertible Model 222K* has a tubular bed that is exposed by loosening a screw and removing its extension plate assembly. And it has a throw-out device to keep the feed dog from working while sewing with the extension plate off.

Mowry Photo

Model 222K - extension plate removed

Because of these special features, the 222K weighs about one pound more than the regular black 221 or 221K (12 pounds, 3 ounces = 5.6 kg). Otherwise, it's virtually identical to the common *Featherweight* machine. *Singer* advertised that it was particularly suitable for working on sleeves, cuffs and pant legs; also for setting zippers, and monogramming pockets and cuffs. It was made for the woman who planned to do a lot of darning and embroidery. The machine is quite rare and it commands a corresponding high value, particularly from collectors.

Fact is usually more fascinating than fiction because fiction can be created with words, repetition or with the ease of a keyboard in the format of a serious article. But facts are accurate accountings of something; and from an historical or technical perspective they take time to research and confirm. Let me illustrate using the 222K machine as an example. While on the quilt teaching circuit I've often heard that this Free Arm machine was never marketed in the U.S. because a Swiss Company held the U.S. Patent on the free arm design. So - the story goes - every single 222K was originally sold in Canada and British Commonwealth countries. Fact or fiction? Well in this case it's fiction; the 222K was most certainly sold in the U.S. The sales statistics are shown later in this section. Here's another example. I have a reference that shows on good authority that the very first 222K Free Arm machine was built at Clydebank in 1952. This first machine is reported to have serial number EK 637884. But I know from research that EK prefix machines were first manufactured in November, 1954. So in this instance the years don't correspond. Then, just recently I received a letter from a woman in New Zealand telling how she found a 222K at the local weekly auction and, happily, was able to buy it. She wrote that this machine has a serial number of EJ 621467, corresponding to a birthdate in late 1953 or, more likely, early 1954. The machine's EJ serial number prefix indicates it was made earlier than the EK serial number that was reported by the reference source for the very first 222K Free Arm machine ever built. These are examples of the interesting twists and turns one sees in *Featherweight* collecting - at times the available data is contradictory - although much of this is of real value only to historians and collectors. All of the 222K Free Arm machines

I've seen had serial number prefixes of EJ through ER, representing the years 1954 into 1960.

One of the most frequently asked questions is - how many Free Arm machines were made? We can do some figuring. Factory marketing figures I've obtained from *Singer's* archives show that only 1267 machines were sold in the U.S. between 1954 and the first quarter of 1959. All of these *222K Convertibles* were manufactured at the Clydebank factory in Scotland; and if this record is authentic (I believe it is) the 1267 unit figure represents almost all of the 222K sales in the States. Now, let's compare this sales figure with the 1,080,000 regular *Model 221 Featherweights* that were manufactured at the U.S. Elizabethport factory during this same five plus year span. In net, the domestic sale of *Featherweight* Free Arm machines accounts for a tiny percentage of that total.

For those of you interested in the details, figures from the archived sales record are reproduced here:

> 1954 - 290 machines
> 1955 - 276
> 1956 - 210
> 1957 - 153
> 1958 - 311
> 1959 - 27
>
> Total = 1267 = U.S. sales from Jan. '54 through March '59

I think it's reasonable to assume that a few additional Free Arm machines were sold in the U.S. from April of '59, to the end of 1960 at the latest. Using an average annual sales figure since 1954, I've concluded that no more than 1800 Free Arm machines were ever sold domestically.

But what about the sales of 222K Free Arm machines outside of the States? I've reviewed extensive serial number and owner location records, along with the correspondence I have. About four times as many machines are reported from Canada and

British Commonwealth locations, as compared with U.S. owners. (This data is accurate as I write it today, but the database continues to evolve.) With this we can roughly estimate the total production of the 222K Free Arm machine.

Sales of the 222K outside of the U.S. may be calculated with fair accuracy by multiplying the U.S. sales figure (1800 machines) by four. So with this, I am proposing that some 7200 Free Arm *Featherweights* were originally sold elsewhere in the world markets.

Now, let's keep figuring. 1800 (U.S.) plus 7200 (outside U.S.) suggests a production figure of about 9,000 for these elusive 222K *Featherweight Convertible* sewing machines. Let's call it 10,000 just to be safe. This represents only <u>about one third of one percent</u> of the total production of *Featherweights*. Now I know why 222K's are so rare, much more so than related by references and machine collectors.

Another question I'm often asked is why the 222K Free Arm machine was discontinued. The low production figure should answer this one, but let's go back to 1948 for more insight. The first U.S. free arm machine was made that year by the Portman Manufacturing Company of New Rochelle, New York. Although it had the tubular bed feature, zigzag machines were starting to come in vogue. So the straight-stitch Portman met with limited demand. Within a year or two, a Swiss-made machine started to appear. It had a free arm and a zigzag, and the Portman's fate was sealed. Similarly with the 222K. I'd say the demand just wasn't high enough, in part because it couldn't do a zigzag.

Looking backwards I guess the gremlins really didn't need much help to do their work. Finding a Free Arm *Featherweight* is much like looking for the proverbial needle in a haystack!

CHAPTER TEN

LIMITED EDITIONS

In this section I'll write about the more rarely seen machines - those that exist in fact rather than fiction. And I'll leave the fictional ones for a later chapter. The machines here are presented in order by year of introduction.

1934 Century of Progress

This limited edition is the *Featherweight* machine that's usually linked with the 1933 World's Fair that was held in Chicago, Illinois. The Fair opened in May of that year and its theme was "A Century of Progress". Its organizers wanted to look back at the tremendous technical and scientific advances over the preceding century. We had gone from a society that was mainly dependent on individual effort and animal power, to one that had developed such wonders as steam engines, automobiles, airplanes, telephones and radios. I'm not sure if the Fair's theme also related to Chicago's Centennial, but there is some evidence that it did. More to follow on this point. And, as I wrote earlier in this book, The *Singer Sewing Company* chose to introduce its new Featherweight portable sewing machine at this 1933 World's Fair.

On the 1934 Century of Progress machine the regular *Singer* medallion that's riveted to the front of its arm was replaced with one that says "Century of Progress" at the top of the oval, and "Chicago, 1934" at the bottom. These words are in gold letters on a wine-colored ring, with the *Singer* logo and trademark legend in gold in the center of the medallion. Now for my theory. The 1933 World's Fair did have the Century of Progress theme, but it opened and closed in 1933. And the medallion clearly says: Chicago, 1934. Accordingly, I believe the Century of Progress *Featherweight* edition commemorated both the World's Fair and Chicago's Centennial, which was probably held in 1934. I presume they were sold by company stores and salesmen mainly in the Chicago area in the 1934-35 time frame. It is an extremely rare machine edition.

I have never personally seen one of these 1934 Century of Progress machines, but I did have a woman from California write and send pictures of hers. It has serial number AD 721441, with a birthdate of September 10, 1934. She and her husband are lucky owners, considering its rarity. Only a small portion of the series AD machines with the September 10, 1934 birthdate had the special Century of Progress medallion, and they seem to be intermixed with others in the production run. Another woman wrote to me saying she owned a *Featherweight* that was bought at the 1933 World's Fair in Chicago. I wrote back and asked for pictures and serial number information. Her response disappointed both of us! The machine was a British made series FA machine that was made in about 1970. She was told the World's Fair story when she inherited the machine that was formerly owned by a relative. Apparently someone in the family had created another legend. At least we were able to clear it up!

1936 Texas Centennial Exposition

Several years ago I was teaching in Utah and a woman in class told me she owned a special *Featherweight* machine that was marked "Texas Centennial Exposition - 1836-1936" on its medallion. Unfortunately, she didn't have the machine with her that day, and we never did connect later. But I made note of it while in class and I'm including it here to be complete. Some limited research showed that Texas did hold an Independence Centennial Exposition in the Spring of 1936, but I wasn't able to find out its location nor details. I've heard that the *Singer* Model 201 was introduced there. I presume all of these 1936 Texas Centennial 221's are series AE machines. At this point I do not know how many were made. But they have to be very rare.

1939 Golden Gate Exposition - San Francisco

The Golden Gate Exposition edition had a special medallion that reads "Golden Gate Exposition" at the top, and "San Francisco 1939" on the bottom. I have a single correspondent who reports having one. The owner is from California and he wrote that this series AF machine with its birthdate of October 10, 1938 is one of his rare ones. Production data is lacking on this special edition as well.

1939-40 Black Crinkle Finish 221

One of the more curious *Featherweight* editions is the machine that's finished in crinkle, matte, or wrinkle black. I've heard all these terms used to describe its paint, which is dull black with a rough texture. (For the sake of simplicity I'll use black crinkle throughout this section). And that's not all! This *Model 221* has two sets of grooves, with three parallel grooves in each set, that are cast into its bed and swinging bed extension. They run lengthwise with the machine. The grooves are set in, or indented, beginning about one half inch from the front and back edges of the machine. Each groove is about 1/8-inch wide and 1/32-inch in depth. There are no fancy gold trim decals, and the grooves lie about where the bed decals would be. Serial number data indicates these machines had 1939-40 birthdates. Some of them have a flat metal face plate (unlike any others) that was painted to match the machine. Still others I've seen have the striated face plate, which was not introduced until 1947. A real mystery! Otherwise, the machine is a standard *Model 221* with the later, numbered-dial tension adjustment. The handwheel even shows its lineage, with the regular black japan finish. So what is it, you ask!

Donna and Arnold Poster

Model 221 Black Crinkle Finish

This question has intrigued owners and collectors alike since *Featherweights* moved to preeminence over the past few years. A man from Maryland who has repaired sewing machines for thirty years was told they were made during the War when good paint was hard to get, but he said he couldn't swear to this. The prevalent theory is that it's a military version of the machine. The black crinkle type of finish suggests use where light reflection from shiny surfaces might be a problem. This is an apparent link to our military services with their olive drab, battleship gray, and camouflage color schemes. However, this theory is widely and I must say jokingly disparaged. *Featherweights* in combat? Hardly!

After considerable study, I've concluded that the black crinkle 221 <u>is in fact</u> a federal contract version, probably military. Most everything the military buys is a drab color, whether intended for use in combat or not. The black crinkle finish was surely specified in the contract; it wasn't merely a situation where good paint was hard to get. A period <u>Singer</u> Parts Manual I have refers to their Type P.P. style of finish - which is described as "Wrinkle Finish". This may be the official name of the black crinkle.

No, I don't think this *Featherweight* was used in front line foxholes. But there were certainly applications for portable sewing machines in the military, such as clothing repairs in field camps and posts. The real clincher though are those parallel grooves. I've studied and studied these machines. If the grooves have a practical sewing purpose I haven't found it! Then it came to me. Simply, I believe that the grooves were specified in the contract to discourage people from taking government property. And if someone did, the grooved machine would be immediately suspect at *Singer* repair centers because they were not available commercially. Why not just stamp the machine with a legend like: U.S. Property? Probably because the stamp mark could be filled in with black paint, or even filed off. Those grooves were just too imposing!

My research shows there are two distinct serial number ranges of these black crinkle machines, all in the AF series (1939-40).

This suggests two contract orders, or possibly, two separate shipments on the same contract. The big question is why some of these machines had striated face plates when that type wasn't introduced until later on in 1947. This can be confusing to folks who compare features against serial number and birthdate records.

A couple in Texas own a black crinkle machine with serial number AF 387847. This machine has a birthdate of December 5, 1939. It has the crinkle finish as described previously, along with a simple flat face plate that has three tiny grooves that run vertically and are roughly centered. The face plate is painted to match the machine. This machine appears to be from the first contract run.

Another black crinkle machine I've seen is owned by a man in Maine. It's also a series AF machine, serial number AF 589268, with a birthdate of August 15, 1940 - which I believe was the second run. However, it has the regular circa 1947 shiny striated faceplate. I suppose this later type face plate could have been retrofitted by a former owner to improve the looks of the machine; but I'm aware of several other machines in the same serial number range that also have this striated face plate. This is a bit of a mystery.

A plausible explanation is that there was an overrun of the special grooved machine beds in 1939 for the first contract order. These beds were serial numbered during the machining process, and were placed in storage awaiting future orders - because (of the grooves) they could not be fitted to the regular commercial machines. Then, during 1941-45 *Singer's* precision tooling was needed for the nation's defense. The company moved to production of handguns and other wartime commodities. Production of sewing machines was essentially nil over this entire period. To complete this scenario, a second federal contract order was filled in 1947, and the special grooved beds and extension plates were hauled out of storage and used along with the regular striated face plate which was then in production. This would account for the mix of pre and post-war parts on some of the black crinkle 221 machines. At this point my theory sounds good but I can't certify it completely.

To be complete with information let me say I've heard that some of these machines were supplied with military olive drab colored carrying cases, complete with stenciled military spec numbers. I have never seen one of these cases, and I've been unable to get a photo of one. In fact, all of the crinkle machine cases I've seen or have photos of are the regular black leatherette type. This military color information is suspect at best.

Also, here's some trivia relating to the military that I learned from a *Featherweight* collector in Michigan. He sent me a sketch of a medical instrument that used a *Featherweight* bobbin. He wrote that it was used for "First Aid" in combat (to sew up wounds), and that medics were trained in its use. I thank God on behalf of our service people that medical technology has advanced since the forties!

I don't know how many black crinkle 221 machines were made. They were probably sold as surplus when no longer useful for government purposes. Serial number records show that at least 150 machines were in the first run with the 1939 birthdate. The apparent second run, those with the 1940 birthdate, is less clear though. The range of serial numbers on reported machines is small so I won't even venture a guess. Let me say, however, that only six out of the seven hundred plus people who have written to me can lay claim to own a black crinkle machine. And I've only seen two of them in quilting classes across the country. They have to be relatively scarce.

Blackside Machines
Moving into the World War Two era, we find another interesting variant. These black-colored *221 Featherweight* machines made very limited use of the shiny plating normally found on parts such as the face plate, presser foot, the hand wheel rim and other smaller parts. These parts were normally electroplated using a single process with nickel, or a double process with nickel and chromium. However, Both metals are needed to make high tensile alloy steels such as used in gears and ordnance. And while the U.S. was not at war when some of these machines were made, it was helping its allies

and making preparations itself. Nickel and chromium were being tightly controlled, and availability for civilian products like sewing machines was limited. The U.S. Mint was even forced to make the 1942-45 Jefferson Nickel out of almost pure silver, because silver was more available than the nickel alloy used in 5-cent coins! Later, after the war, nickel and chromium were still in short supply for some time before parts could revert to shiny plating. But the plated handwheel rim never did return to the line. Most all U.S. machines made since the war show its legacy through their black-painted wheel rims.

The early "blackside" *Featherweights* were supplied with the second-type scrollwork faceplates and handwheel rims which were coated or painted black. Also, the presser foot may or may not be black. I don't know for sure what the actual scrollwork finish was, but a period Singer parts manual refers to their X style of finish, described as "black oxide for iron and steel". This sounds like a chemical process and it may be what was used. Serial number records show these early blacksides began to be seen sporadically in early 1941. Some examples may have a mix of plated and black coated parts, indicating use of warehouse parts inventory.

Another version, after the war, used a simple punched steel face plate that was painted black to match the machine's regular black japan finish. Again, the handwheel rim was black. The latter type of face plate is similar to the one supplied many years later on the 221K5, 221J6 and the 221K7 machines. When the punched steel type was supplied, a different face plate retaining screw was used. It has a shiny teardrop-shaped head.

Let me tell you about two examples of the earlier machine. A woman in New York owns a black *Featherweight* with serial number AG 013110. Its birthdate is July 1, 1941. It is original and exactly as described here. Likewise with the AG 013403 machine owned by a couple in Michigan. This second machine even has black attachments and bobbins, witnessing increased shortages of nickel and chromium due to government needs.

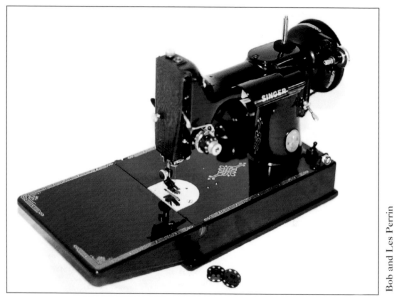

Model 221 Blackside (early)

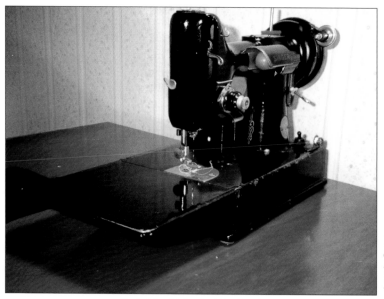

Model 221 Blackside (late)

A good example of a younger or post-war blackside machine is owned by a woman in California. It has serial number AG 883740, with a birthdate of November 22, 1946. The machine appears to be "all original" with black pressed steel face plate, teardrop head retaining screw and black handwheel rim. It does have the regular shiny plated presser foot.

It appears that comparatively few blackside machines were made. We can estimate production to some extent for the pre-war version. The earliest one I have heard of is serial number AG 011747, owned by a woman from New York with whom I've corresponded. There are some 1650 machine serial numbers between this one and the machine owned by the Michigan couple. However, the complete range of serial numbers is not known at this time.

The second type, the one with the black pressed steel face plate, seems to be the least common of the two versions. I've personally seen only the one machine I reported here; and have heard of only two others in all of my teaching travels. Therefore, I don't have enough data to estimate production. But they must be very rare. I'm hoping that more examples will come to light in the near future.

Singer Centennial Model - U.S. Machines

I've received more than a few letters over the years that referenced the "United States Centennial" model of the *Featherweight*. Some other letters referred to the "Bi-Centennial" model. Both are incorrect. Yes, there was a Centennial model of the *Model 221* but it had nothing to do with an anniversary of our country. This special *Featherweight* machine commemorated Singer's Centennial in the business of manufacturing sewing machines. Its century started in 1851 after Isaac Singer perfected the first practical sewing machine.

A few years earlier, Elias Howe, Jr. studied his wife's hand movements while sewing and went on to invent and patent (1846) the first lock-stitch sewing device. However, the invention wasn't practical because it sewed vertically, and it didn't have a mechanism to feed the fabric. If the seam was longer than could be sewn in one movement, its operator had to stop the machine again and again to re-position the fabric. Isaac Singer took this concept and created a machine to sew horizontally, and to continuously feed and sew until one of the two stitching threads ran out. This was in 1850, and apparently the *Singer* company was launched in 1851.

Centennial machines started to appear in the mid-range of Series AJ in early 1950, probably in anticipation of 1951 which was the actual centennial year. Production was very strong through 1951 and into machine Series AK. The last machines seem to be birthdated in the AK 7 to 800000 range in early 1952.

This Centennial version is the regular black-color machine, with a special brass medallion on its arm that has a blue trim ring. Within the blue trim it reads: "A CENTURY OF SEWING SERVICE" at the top, and "1851 (star) 1951" at the bottom. The brass center of the medallion reads: "THE SINGER MANFG. CO.". The machine was probably intended as a prestige model, and so it is even today. Women in class who have a Centennial (or so-called Anniversary) machine usually mention it to their classmates.

Mowry Photo

U.S. Model 221 - Centennial Edition

And many people who have written to me make note that theirs is the Centennial or Anniversary edition. They do command somewhat higher prices when being sold. I don't know how many were made. Although they are not particularly rare, they are not all that common either. Remember they were only made for about two years. All told, they are one of the scarcer machines.

Singer **Centennial Model - British Machines**

Singer's 1951 Centennial was also commemorated through a special edition of the Clydebank 221K1 machine. These British-made Centennials began to be seen at the mid-point of Series EF in late 1949. And production continued into about the middle of Series EG in 1951. The latest machine I'm currently aware of is owned by a woman in Massachusetts who bought it in Dublin, Ireland in 1951. It has serial number EG 545587, with a birthdate in mid-1951. It's possible that newer machines will be reported as time goes on. However, I own the serial number EH 132853 machine (birthdate February 29, 1952) and it is not a Centennial model. Apparently the edition was terminated at Clydebank sometime during 1951.

The Centennial medallion on the black 221K machine is identical to the one used on the U.S. Centennial machine - brass center, trimmed in blue, with the same legend as described previously. However, there are some differences between the machines. All of the Centennial British-made *Featherweights* seem to be the 221K4 version, with the toggle-type switch on the right end of the light fixture. Also, every one I've seen had the second version of the scrollwork face plate. In comparison, the Centennial U.S. machines have light switches in the usual place on top of the machine bed, and all seem to have the striated face plate.

Let me spin an interesting tale on a particular British Centennial machine that was owned by a woman in New York. We first corresponded back in 1993. She had a Centennial model with a scrollwork face plate and a 230-250 volt motor, having bought it in England before moving to the States. A replacement motor wasn't to be had so she used the machine as a bookend. She also collects sewing tools so she took off the little *Singer* plate (the Centennial medallion) to add to her collection. Then she offered the machine to me - to be used to give new life to some of my students' machines. I filed the letter away along with many others. Then, just recently while teaching in Ohio I came across a British "parts machine" (not a Centennial model). I remembered the letter and asked my husband to call. The bookend was still in New York but now it was missing its bobbin case. Not to worry - the parts machine had them. All told, we were able to get the two of them together and come up with one working machine. My husband said it was like a phoenix coming back for sewing duty. Incidentally, the new owner loves it!

Centennial Medallion

Mowry Photo

There is a bit of a mystery with these British Centennial machines. Some of them were originally sold in the States, while U.S. Centennials were being made and sold at the same time. Here's one example. A woman from Alabama owns a machine that was purchased by a tailor in 1952. She wrote that he sewed for the public and paid for it by working for just two weekends! Later he went to Korea and carried this machine with him. She supposed he repaired military uniforms. Anyway, this machine has serial number EG 079798 (Clydebank) and was purchased new in Wilmington, North Carolina.

The occurrence of these British Centennial machines is definitely less than their U.S. Centennial counterparts. Again, they seem to command somewhat premium prices when offered for sale.

221K5 Black-Colored Featherweight

The 221K5 British machine is easily identified by its pressed steel face plate and special bobbin winder that has a projection for your finger. It was introduced in (about) 1961 in the ES serial number series. Although there is a prevalent belief that all 221K5 machines were beige in color (the 221J model), a very few were apparently finished in the regular japan black. I received several photos of one of these black-colored machines about three years ago. It appeared to be authentic; maybe it was a sales prototype for the beige-color 221J production machine. But then again, it may have been a counterfeit - a 221J that was repainted black. However, the 221J is itself a comparatively rare machine, so why would anyone do that? Unfortunately, though, the photos and their accompanying letter were misplaced in the process of cataloging all of my correspondence. So I don't have a serial number to reference. I'll confess that I thought about neglecting to mention it here, but that omission would be a disservice to *Featherweight* owners and collectors. So, hopefully, an example or two of this black japan finished 221K5 will come to light in the near future. Anyone that owns one is going to find that she/he has a mighty rare machine.

Mowry Photo

Model 221J Featherweight

Bureau of Indian Affairs - 1961

About three years ago I learned about what was probably a special contract purchase of *Featherweights,* in a letter from a woman in Arizona. She was the owner of Model 221K that was marked "Bureau of Indian Affairs". After some correspondence I learned that the machine was beige in color, had serial number ES 874171, and was indeed a model 221J. It was originally purchased from an Apache American Indian woman who also lived in Arizona, and it had a metal plate attached to its bed that read:

> Department of Interior
> (property number)
> Bureau of Indian Affairs

This machine has a birthdate of August 19, 1961. The metal plate appears to have been added by *Singer* or by Bureau employees, after the machine was built. I was intrigued that its property number (which I deliberately omitted in the inset above) was in the mid-two thousands. Now, I don't know if some 2500 sewing machines were purchased by the Bureau for use by American Indian women. Or - to tantalize you *Featherweight* collectors - if about 2500 Bureau-marked 221J machines were out there back in the early sixties. It's an interesting point to ponder.

Blue-tinted Featherweight 221K7

This is another one that may exist! As mentioned in Chapter 5, I've heard of a blue-tinted version of the 221K7. You'll recall this is the late British edition of the *Featherweight* with its short (3 1/2-inch) swinging bed extension. Three reputable service men have written to me reporting that they've seen one. One man said its color was named something like "turquoise" - he didn't remember for sure, but he did describe a light blue tint in its white paint. Then a Michigan couple wrote, saying how my first *Featherweight* book sparked an old flame of interest in that little machine. They began actively searching for them. Along the way they called *Singer's* Customer Relations Department and were told that the [Featherweight] machine was made in . . . . light blue.

I have seen literally hundreds of white, bisque and green (barely celery) 221K7's in class, but I've never come across a blue-tinted one. However, at this point there is enough credible evidence for me to keep me looking for light blue-tinted 221K7. The jury is still out on this one!

CHAPTER ELEVEN

FACT OR FICTION?

I'll admit that I've looked forward to writing a chapter on Featherweight legends and myths. Yes - I've come across many of them relating to the classic machine while traveling the quilt teaching circuit. Still others came to me in letters from correspondents. Some of the tales of unusual Model 221 variants have surprising tenacity. They are quoted and requoted so much that they become "fact". To say otherwise is like insulting motherhood or disliking apple pie. No Featherweights have been subject to more discussion and debate than the ones in this chapter.

I didn't pretend to know the answers to start. I listened intently to anyone talking about Featherweights. And I remembered or took notes on what I heard. I started to research actual machine records, looked for reliable accounts by owners, and searched for factory literature to help confirm or deny the legends. Also, I thought that service and repair people would be untapped sources of good information. Many of them saw more Model 221's in one week than others see in a lifetime. Okay, maybe some of you think that I'm a skeptic, a person who needs to see something or hear all of the details to believe. But my profession demands it! Attention to detail is essential in quilt making, teaching and writing on technical subjects.

After starting research for the first edition of this book, I had feelings of doubt on some of the stories. Intense study since then has firmed up some, and discounted others. Yes, I found that some of the tales of unusual models and variations were fact. I've documented these in the preceding chapters. In other cases, though, I have serious reservations so I believe that certain legends are dubious at best. These latter are discussed in this chapter.

Magnesium Featherweight

There's a legend that the bed and arm of some of the U.S. post-war *Featherweights* were made out of magnesium rather than aluminum. For those of you unfamiliar with magnesium, it's a silvery metal that is only about two-thirds as heavy as aluminum. Its chemical symbol is Mg (keep this in mind). Magnesium is normally used in alloys with aluminum and other metals, and in the post-war era they were the lightest structural alloys in common use.

If this story was accurate, some of the Series AG and AH machines should weigh at least two pounds less than their aluminum counterparts. Nine instead of eleven pounds would be about right. Yes, I've weighed many of these machines but haven't found any "nine pounders" as yet. I also have to wonder why *Singer* would choose to manufacture a machine from a more exotic alloy that would cost a lot more than common aluminum. The only practical reasons would be that aluminum was scarce at the time (it wasn't), or that they wanted to manufacture an "Ultra-Featherweight". I haven't found any period literature so far that advertised such a creation.

Where did this story come from? I'll take a wild shot in the dark. Please refer back to Chapter 3 and the White Sewing Machine Company's machine called the "Featherweight Portable type in the Luggage Case". Remember that it was marketed in the post-war era and was called their Model 77MG. The regular machine was the Model 77. The similarity of its MG model suffix and the Mg chemical symbol struck me as curious. Is it possible this machine was made out of a magnesium alloy to achieve its light weight? And further, that its Featherweight name was confused with the *Singer Featherweight*? Unfortunately though, I've never seen a White Company's Model 77MG Featherweight sewing machine so I have no way of proving this theory.

Possibly some readers can shed more light on this one. But for now I'll have to conclude that the *Singer Featherweight Model 221* was never made out of magnesium.

Red-colored Featherweight

I heard this legend years ago. The story is that *Singer* made some special versions of the *Featherweight* for gifts to Dealers who sold a lot of machines. The tale doesn't mention whether they were U.S. or British machines, early or late manufacture - just that they were *Featherweights.* But to date, I haven't heard of anyone who's been able to come up with a bona-fide example of this red-colored *Model 221.* Also, I've checked with many former *Singer* sales, service and repair people, and no one has ever seen one. But many had heard the oft-repeated story of the red-colored machine.

Additional data came from a very knowledgeable correspondent in California who wrote that *Singer* did not have dealerships prior to 1963. Its machines could only be purchased from *Singer* company-owned stores or Singer employees. So the bit in the legend about presentation to Dealers doesn't make sense . . . . unless the alleged red *Featherweights* were the late 221K7 British machines which began to be seen in 1964.

Personally, I think it's a case of confusion with another sewing machine model - although red is an unusual color for any sewing machine. The most likely possibility is that the mythical red *Featherweight* is actually the red-colored miniature sewing machine that was made by Singer. This is their No. 20 machine and it seems that it was called (believe it or not) the Sew Handy.

A man in Pennsylvania sent me a photo of three of these miniature machines; they were hand-powered and he said they were desirable Singer models highly sought by collectors. There was one each of <u>red</u>, gray and blue. Then a woman in Michigan mailed a photo of this same miniature machine, but this one was black and it even had a small luggage-type case. Her photo caption indicates the machine is a - Singer Toy Sewhandy. Needless to say, these letters sparked my interest. I did more research and found that the red miniature is listed as *Singer's* No. 20 machine.

Although they are often called toys, the No. 20 Sew Handy machine was primarily intended to "teach little girls to sew, [although] they are used by many college and business girls for occasional mending and altering". There was an electric model which weighed less than six pounds. The hand model weighed even less and was said to be very light running. In 1960, the Sew Handy No. 20-10 retailed for $8.95. This is the hand operated version. And its Carrying Case retailed for $4.50 East and only 50 cents more in the West!

Singer® "Toy" Sew Handy

Putting all this together I don't believe there was ever a genuine red-colored *Featherweight*. The most plausible explanation is that Singer's red-colored No. 20 miniature machine is actually the mythical red *Featherweight*.

Green-colored and Blue-colored Featherweights

Ever since I became interested in *Featherweights* I've heard that green and blue-colored versions were made. But no one seemed to have one, although most everyone into *Model 221's* had heard about them. Then, after writing the first edition of this book, I started getting calls and letters from folks who claimed to own one, or at least to have some information on them. Early on, my heart usually stopped! This is it, I thought. At last I'll be able to see one of those machines! But it never happened. As time went on I began to become somewhat of a skeptic. And today, I don't believe either one was ever made.

Some of the "green machine" contacts made sense right off. *Singer* did make the British 221K7 machine in what they called "green" - although it was really white with a green tint. And as I wrote in an earlier chapter, this color should be more accurately called "barely celery". However, still others insisted that they (or their friend in many instances) owned or knew about a true green-color *Featherweight Model 221*. I just had to see one!

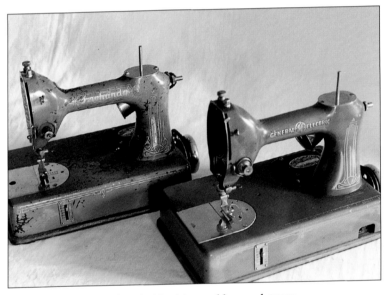

Sewhandy Machines - blue and green

Similarly with the reports of blue-color *Featherweights*. A turquoise or light blue version of the 221K7 British machine may have been made in small numbers, as I proposed in the preceding chapter. However . . . . I've never actually seen one in person or through a photo. But several folks told me that they or an acquaintance had seen a darker, true blue-color version of the regular Model 221. I wanted to believe they were out there!

I wrote or asked for pictures and more details. Several people took pains to send me photos, but they proved to be green or blue-colored *Sewhandy* machines, mistaken for *Singer Featherweights*! Remember that they were available in several colors including "larch green" and "marine blue"? I extended thanks for the efforts - in some cases the owners realized that their machine wasn't a *Featherweight* after writing to me, but they honored my request anyway just to clear up the matter. This is commendable. Also, it's understandable how a green or blue-colored *Sewhandy* (whether Standard, Ossan or General Electric) could be mistaken for a genuine *Featherweight*, especially when placed in its regular black luggage case. It sure looks like one!

Other people never responded to my inquiry and I assumed that their green or blue sewing machine wasn't really a *Featherweight*. Or, it may be that they were unable to give me any additional details on the machine they reported. So far, I was drawing a big ZERO, and admittedly, I started to become skeptical about the green and blue rumors. I began to think - these legends can't be just based on green or blue Sewhandys being mistaken for *Featherweights* - there has to be something else. Yes, I believe there is! Simply, some other *Singer* machine models have been (and are) mistaken for *Featherweights*.

A Pennsylvania woman who worked for *Singer* for seven years wrote to me about the 185K and 185J three-quarter head machines, which were green. She had customers refer to them as their "Featherweights" although they were far from being featherweight because they were made of heavy cast iron. She said the 185's were sold as portables because they were smaller in size than the standard head. (One of my references places the 185K/J machines in the 1960-62 time frame.) More information on the "green machine" confusion came from a man in Massachusetts who is a sewing machine mechanic. He wrote that he runs across many machines that are mistaken for the *Featherweight*. He said the green one is in fact the Singer 99 model, a three-quarter [head] version of the *Singer 66*.

Remember the blue *Singer* Toy Sewhandy that I mentioned earlier in this chapter on the Red-colored machine legend? I have a photo of one of these miniature machines in blue. Yes - it is a small portable Singer machine that came with a luggage-type case. It could help account for the legend of the blue-color *Featherweight*.

The bottom line is that I do not believe that any true green or true blue-colored *Featherweight Model 221* machines were ever made. It appears the tales of these machines are based on confusion with the earlier *Sewhandy* portable sewing machines, or with other *Singer* portables and miniature sewing machines.

To underscore the point I'll share one more experience. A very few days after writing the manuscript for this section I received a call from a woman who told me she read my book, and she had the elusive green machine. I asked if she was sure it was a *Singer Featherweight*. Yes. She promised to send photos. When my husband came home I told him I might have to change my manuscript. The photos arrived about two weeks later . . . . no, I didn't have to change this chapter. It was another green *General Electric* Sewhandy machine with its black carrying case. The letter said it was the machine I wanted to find.

Brown-colored machines

I have never seen a brown-colored *Singer Featherweight* and I haven't come across anyone that has. But the legend persists. And the brown-color in this legend is not just a terminology confusion with the beige (tan) color of the Model 221J machines. Folks report it as brown! Simply, I don't believe that any brown-color *Featherweights* were ever made by *Singer*. But I'll propose a possible candidate to account for this myth.

I think it's the brown-color "Featherweight portable" that was made in the post-war era by the White Sewing Machine Company - the Model 77MG. It even came with a small luggage-type carrying case like the one for the *(Singer) Featherweight*. I've written about this machine previously. And I suspect it accounts for legend of the brown-color *Singer Featherweight 221*.

CHAPTER TWELVE

FEATHERWEIGHT CARRYING CASE

F*eatherweights* were supplied with a luggage type carrying case that was intended for storage at home, and ease and security while traveling. The case locked, and the machine could not bounce or shift back and forth once its top or lid was closed. There were several variations of this case. All of them were well designed and built for years of use.

I'll start out with a comment on "originality". Many carrying cases are not original to their current resident machines. Loss, and replacement due to wear and tear, have left many *Featherweights* with carrying cases that are younger or older than their machine series code would seem to indicate.

Type One Carrying Case

Dale Pickens and Bob's Picture Box

Type One (black)

The very earliest *Featherweights* came with a carrying case that looks remarkably like the one supplied by *Standard* with its *Sewhandy* machines. They may have been made for *Singer* by the same supplier. This *Featherweight* case has a black leatherette covering and a bluish green interior lining. Its handle is covered with black leather and it has two key-lockable latches made of solid brass. Brass was also used for the hinges and the handle keepers. The special *Singer* oil can was held in place by a metal clip at the bottom of the case, on top of the cleat that located the end of the machine with the swinging bed extension.

Its lift-out accessory tray also has the bluish green covering, but there are two variations of this tray. On the earliest one, the far right floor of the tray is cut out, and it has a metal clip to hang the foot controller (all metal) in the machine compartment. A black metal V brace is attached to the case lid - when closed it rests on the neck of the machine head to prevent movement when carrying. This tray was used for a short time in 1933-35, when it was modified somewhat. The cut-out in the floor was eliminated and some minor changes were made to the layout of its compartments. The V brace on the case lid was gone. The tray now had a full floor, and was designed for convenient storage of the foot controller, thread, needles, spare bobbins in a holder, the machine attachment set (loose), and a tube of *Singer* motor lubricant.

Although there are two variations of the removable accessory trays, I don't try to differentiate between them when referring to the carrying case. Simply, I call the case with the bluish green insides the Type One carrying case.

For the sake of comparison let's talk about the *Sewhandy* carrying case. Most of them were black (a very few were made in brown). It has a gold-color lining, a removable tray, and two simple brass latches, along with a third key-lockable center latch. Its accessory tray looks like the first variation of the Type One described here, except for color. And both cases have the same type of reinforced inside corners, using wooden moldings that have a triangle cross-section. Case lengths and widths are about the same, and the *Sewhandy* case is only about 3/4-inch shorter in height. It's hard to tell one from the other at more than a few feet. Sounds like the *Featherweight* carrying case design was also influenced by the *Sewhandy*, doesn't it?

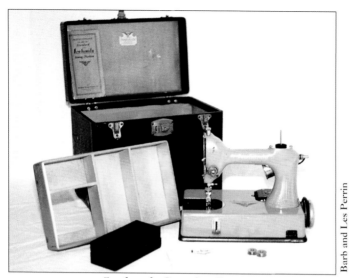

Sewhandy Carrying Case

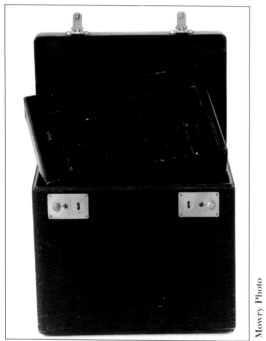

Type Two Carrying Case

Type Two (black)
Later, in (about) 1935 by the start of machine series AE, the lift-out tray was changed from bluish green to black. The lining of the carrying case went to black as well. Also, the case latches became larger, with spring-loaded top halves. And the latches, hinges and handle attachments were changed to aluminum trim. Otherwise, this case is similar to the Type One.

Sizing is the same: 13-inches by 8-inches by 11 1/2-inches high. (I didn't include the handle in the height measurement.) Its handle is still covered with black leather. I call this carrying case the Type Two and its part number is 45832. After its introduction, the case was supplied with *Featherweight* machines into the mid-point of machine series AJ in 1950.

Type Three (black)

Machines that are birthdated after mid-1950 in series AJ were supplied with the Type Three case. This is *Singer's* Model 270 - part number 45911, and it was the last version of the black-colored carrying case. It is similar to the Type Two except it doesn't have the removable accessory tray that fits above the machine. So the case is somewhat shorter, i.e., not as tall. Size is 14 1/4-inches by 8-inches by 11-inches high (handle not included).

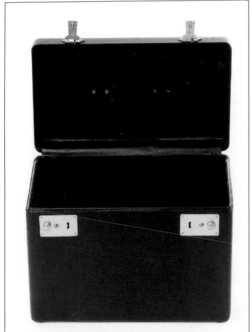

Type Three Carrying Case

Instead of the lift-out accessory tray, there's a metal compartment inside the case, on its left side, that's intended for needles, thread, etc. It has a slot on its extreme left that will hold about eight bobbins. I've seen many women store their small green box of machine attachments in this side compartment, but *Singer* wanted the box to be stored on top of the locating cleat in the left bottom of the case. Most (but not all) of these cases have a metal clip located behind the side compartment to hold the special Singer oil can that had an oval shaped cross-section. However, newer Type Three cases do not have this metal clip. The oil can's shape was changed to the common rectangle cross-section; it was probably easier to manufacture. With these later cases the machine oil can is stored on top of the locating cleat where it cannot scratch the machine's black japan finish.

Since there wasn't a tray to hold the foot controller, it was moved to the inside of the case lid. To lock in place, you slide the controller from right to left inside a metal holder. Do not store the foot controller on top of the machine bed! This practice tends to scratch and chip its black japan finish. Always use the holder inside the case top. Why damage your classic *Featherweight* by saving a few seconds when packing it away?

Incidentally, two kinds of handles were used on the Type Three carrying case. Both are made of black plastic, but one is perfectly smooth, and the other has raised ridges in the center of the handle, probably to provide for a better gripping surface. The smooth one appears to be more common.

221J Carrying Case (beige with brown trim)

The carrying case supplied with the 221J and 221J6 beige-colored *Featherweights* is similar to the Type Three black case in many respects. It has similar dimensions. The side-mounted metal compartment is there, along with the holder inside its top for the foot controller. Also, it doesn't have an oil can retaining clip - because the earlier oval-section type was already obsolete when the J prefix machines were introduced. Once again, the oil can should be stored on top of the cleat to the left of the machine's folded-up bed extension.

221J Carrying Case

A noticeable feature is that the 221J/J6 carrying case has a fancy two-tone color scheme - beige with brown trim strips at the bottom and top of the case, and a brown-colored handle. The inside of the case is mostly beige. Also, there is beige fabric, heavily stitched in place, on top of its lid. Another difference is that the case uses two brass plated steel latches that do not lock.

Mowry Photo

British 221K and 222K Cases (black machines)

Starting in machine series EE, the British black-colored *Featherweights* were supplied with the Type Two carrying case I described previously. This continued into machine series EG (1951 birthdates) when the Type Three case appeared. It was used to the end of production of the 221K black machine in the early nineteen sixties. Also, all 222K *Featherweights* Free Arm machines were supplied with the Type Three case.

I've noted a curiosity with these Type Three carrying cases that were supplied with Clydebank machines. Factory original cases may have latches that are marked "Made in USA" on the back side of their spring-loaded top half. Other cases will have latches with U.K. markings and "Made in England". Those with U.S. legends usually have resident British machines that were imported into Canada for sale in that country or in the States.

Apparently the machines were imported without carrying cases, and were supplied with them after arriving. Likewise, those with U.K. and England legends on their latches typically house black-color machines that were originally sold in the U.K., Australia and New Zealand.

I've had many people ask me to certify that their *Featherweight* is completely "factory original". Anyone with a British black-color 221K or 222K machine can rest assured that USA-marked latches can be original to your carrying case. This simply means the machine was probably an import through our Canadian neighbor.

Lastly, let me say that a very few of the youngest black British *Featherweights* were supplied with a rarely seen carrying case. This case is similar to the 221J carrying case described earlier, except it is cream, with trim strips of taupe (brownish gray) around the top and bottom. I have only seen two of these in my travels and both had early ES series 221K4 machines (light switch on the right end of the light fixture). It appears that this variant was a prototype of the 221J carrying case. I'd speculate that its two-tone color scheme was an attempt to spruce it up and accommodate changing women's tastes.

221K7 Case (green with ivory trim)

The last variation of the *Featherweight* carrying case was supplied with the white or white-tinted British 221K7 machine. This case is "seafoam green" with ivory trim along its top, and it has a matching green-colored handle. The green fabric is heavily stitched to the upper surface of its lid. Inside, it's mostly green. It has only one latch, which is lockable, made of nickel plated steel. The case is shorter than any described previously in this section. It measures 12 1/2-inches by about 8-inches by 10 1/2-inches high (not including the handle). The shorter length was created by eliminating the side compartment for attachments and sewing goodies. Owners are supposed to store the machine attachment set in its box on top of the bed, along with the foot controller

(which was more streamlined than earlier models and permanently wired to the machine). By this time, *Singer* machine oil was being supplied in plastic tubes rather than cans. So the box, controller, and oil could be more or less loose in the case without damaging the machine.

Mowry Photo

221K7 Carrying Case

Musty Odor

One question my earlier edition did not address was how to deal with the musty odor inside some of the carrying cases. I've received many letters on this. A typical one was from a woman in Maryland who wrote that her carrying case has an old musty smell. She had talked with two other Featherweight owners and they had the same problem. She tried cleaning it with several cleaners but had no success in getting rid of it.

I first noticed this problem years ago when I started buying *Featherweight* machines for research. Some carrying cases seemed to be okay, but others had the musty odor. It was particularly common with the older black-colored ones. I called and wrote to previous owners to find out more about the history of my machines. And I learned that the odor is more prevalent with machines that were not used regularly, those that were stored in their cases for months and even years on end. At least that's what it seemed.

I'll tell you about one machine my husband bought. Its black japan finish had some splotches of what looked like mold. Yuk! But a light rubbing with a disinfectant solution (rubber gloves, etc.) took them away and they never came back. The carrying case was another matter though. There was a distinct musty odor whenever I opened it, even after I cleaned the machine. Its black fabric lining looked fine, but I went at it anyway with the disinfectant solution. The odor went away and there was even a mild hint of the disinfectant when the case was opened. Great! I was happy until the musty smell reappeared some months later. Now it was a challenge.

My next step was to expose the open case to bright sunlight. I reasoned that the rays and heat from the summer sun would deodorize its lining. This experiment seemed to go okay, especially when I put my hand on the black lining and found that it was hot to the touch. I kept the case out for two days, moving it from time to time to stay in the direct sunlight. The musty odor was gone! My husband even acknowledged my success. One day he put a hand-drawn sketch in my sewing room showing a *Featherweight* carrying case basking under a benevolent sun; and I must tell you the case had a distinct "happy face" smile penciled on it.

But after several months the musty smell came back! Not as strong as before, but still there. I knew the problem was in the case, behind the lining, but I didn't want to destroy the lining by trying to remove it. So I resorted to a perfume strategy - thinking if I couldn't get rid of the musty odor maybe I could mask it with something more pleasant. I tried several sheets of Bounce perfumed fabric softener, putting them in the bottom of the case beneath the machine. Its subtle perfume masked the musty odor very effectively. This worked so well with the problem case I've written about here that I do it routinely as I bring "new" Featherweights home - whether their cases have a musty odor or not.

Some *Featherweight* owners may want an explanation. A friend who's a microbiologist tells me that mildew causes the musty odor. Mildew spores are all around us in the air, and they need moisture, dark conditions and a nutrient to multiply. All three conditions can be present in carrying cases. But the problem is behind the fabric lining, and it's more or less water resistant. So disinfectant cleaners can't get at it.

Always keep your *Featherweight* machine's carrying case stored away in a low humidity environment. Damp basements or unheated outbuildings are definitely out! This is imperative for the older machines with the black-colored cases. You may not have a problem now, but you don't want one to start. And if you do have the musty smell problem, this will minimize it. Those little packets of desiccants that are packed with computers, cameras, etc. will help too. Put them in the carrying case to absorb moisture that's already there. Also, to minimize smell, try using two or three sheets of Bounce in the bottom of your case to give it a delicate fragrance. Replace occasionally.

Carrying Case Latches
I have seen many of the Type Two and Type Three black carrying cases that have broken latches. They seem to be especially vulnerable. Most frequently, the top half of the latch is completely broken off. This is the spring-loaded part that swings up when it's released. Occasionally, I'll see where the top half of the latch is intact, but its spring is broken. So the latch is lazy and it must be manually pushed up to open the case. A more infrequent problem is a broken spring on the button that releases the swinging top part. The button becomes lazy and it must be pushed left/right with the fingers to release/lock, or to lock/release, depending on which button is broken.

Many people have written to me to find replacement latches. And I was perplexed for years trying to figure out how these case latch top halves are broken off. The latch is certainly well designed, and its swinging top part is made out of solid aluminum. After a bit of experimenting, I found out how.

If you put your *Featherweight* in its carrying case, leave the top open, and then tip it forward - the case will fall on its front. Then, a fraction of a second later the top or lid of the case will drop forward and the tops of both latches will hit the floor with a lot of force. The latch top halves are made of cast aluminum, and one or both are easily broken off. All that you, your child or friend has to do is accidentally tip the case forward, with its top open.

Featherweight owners beware! Replacement latches are not available at present. In the first edition of this book I told how I once bought a nice machine that came in a case that was in good condition except for its latches - both of them were broken off. The previous owner had a piece of ribbon wrapped around the case, tied in a bow. At least it was nice looking, but I was jittery whenever I lifted it because I was expecting the ribbon to break at any second. I couldn't find any suitable replacement latches in my local hardware stores, and I didn't want a common door latch like used on a garage cabinet or shed door, so I appealed to my husband. After quite a few phone calls Frank came to the rescue with a latch that was very similar to the original, nickel plated, which he adapted to the case. It didn't lock, but I didn't really care. We only needed two at that time. But we had to buy one half-gross of them, which was the minimum order quantity.

Well, would you believe that one half-gross lasted less than one year after my first book was released! So many people wrote or called that our entire inventory vanished. We tried to re-order but the latch wasn't available any more.

So you need a latch or a latch spring. What to do? Simply, I don't have a good answer right now. Unlike the *Featherweight* itself where "parts machines" are readily available for scavenging of original parts, "parts carrying cases" aren't out there for things like good used latches. And if you do find a broken case for parts it's difficult to remove the latches. They are held in place with pins that are riveted-over <u>beneath </u>the fabric inside the case. Please don't use a common door latch. Your *Model 221* deserves better than that, and you don't want to detract from its future value. You may be able to find suitable latches in a cabinetry shop. Musical instrument shops are another possibility. If you just need a latch spring, make do by using your fingers to assist the lazy part. Bide your time. At the rate *Featherweight* interest is escalating I believe it's just a matter of time before some enterprising folks offer latch repair services.

Let's say both latches are bad, or you don't have a carrying case at all. My suggestion is to use something else for the time being. Bowling ball bags work well. Also, there are replacement carrying cases on the market right now. They are available in the advertising sections in quilting magazines, or with vendors at the larger quilt shows.

Case Handles

Another common problem are cases that have bad or missing handles. Usually, the plastic ones used in the Type Three carrying cases are in good shape, but the leather covered handles used on earlier cases have a tendency to come apart. My advice is to leave your handle alone unless it's literally in pieces. A worn leather handle has a "distressed" look, plus it's original to the case and the machine. What stories it could tell of its owner's travels through the byways of life. And it looks so much better than one that's wrapped with layers of black plastic electrician's tape.

If you have a handle that's in pieces, there's not much you can do except to repair or replace it. Repair-wise, industrial electrical supply sources have a black-color tubing that can be tightly shrunk in place using a heat source like a heat gun or plumber's torch. Handier people can usually accomplish this sort of work with a little ingenuity. And it's really easy on the earliest version of the leather handle that has D-ring type keepers. Just spread one of the D-rings, slip it over the handle and shrink. Be sure to buy a tube size that's large enough to go over the handle's cross section. Personally, I think this tubing looks better than black plastic tape.

Oftentimes, the carrying case is missing its handle. Don't ask me what happens to them, but I do see a lot without handles - usually the Type One and Type Two versions of the case. Their owners often use a heavy piece of string or twine as an expedient. To my knowledge, an exact replacement leather handle isn't available at present. But who knows in the future? There are similar handles (new) in catalogs right now. While searching flea markets, garage sales and such for *Featherweight* sewing machines, I've seen many similar handles on old luggage, attaché and musical instrument cases. It's absolutely amazing how many handles you'll find when you start looking for them. You or your spouse can show your skill in adapting one to that old Featherweight carrying case.

Other Case Repairs & Maintenance

Occasionally one will see a case with dovetail joints that are coming apart. Repair is a simple matter of re-gluing the bad corner(s) using woodworkers glue, which is available at lumber yards and hardware stores. It seems to work better than the common white liquid glue that's made for general purposes. Then there's loose cover or lining fabric. Loose edges can be glued back in place using any of the better craft glues. General touch-up of scuff marks on black-color cases is best handled with black leather dye or black shoe polish (foam tip, roll-on type) available at supermarkets, etc.

To protect the exterior of the carrying case, I like to use Armor All ® Protectant, which is commonly used on luggage and auto dashboards, panels and seats. For those not familiar with this product, it's sold nationally in automobile and hardware stores. In addition to protecting the leatherette, it adds a sheen that restores the new look of the case.

Lock Keys

One *Singer* key seems to fit the locks on all of the U.S. Type Two and Type Three black-color carrying cases. This key is not interchangeable with the key for British-made carrying cases, although the British key seems to be common for all black-color British cases. And, there is a different key for the seafoam green/ivory trim carrying case supplied with the British 221K7 *Featherweight*. At this point I'm not sure if there's a common key for the Type One cases because they are rarely seen today and I haven't tried enough of them to be certain.

CHAPTER THIRTEEN

FEATHERWEIGHT TABLES and CABINET

No book on the *Singer Featherweight* would be complete without mentioning the famous "Card Table" and the less common "Early American Cabinet". Both were especially designed to fit the *Featherweight* machines and they're part of its odyssey across twentieth century history.

Card Table and Extension Set

The Card Table was officially called the "Folding Utility Table" and (later) the "3-Way Table". It was advertised as a utility table for sewing, card playing and informal dining. *Singer* said it "is an ideal companion to the 221- Portable for the small home or apartment". The table has a removable piece or insert which exposes an opening that allows the machine to sit in and fit flush with the table top; and its surface was rather large for cutting fabric and pinning patterns. The removable insert took the place of the machine when the table was needed for other purposes. When not in use, the Card Table was easy to collapse and store in a closet or room corner. The table had an attractive birch veneer top, stained and varnished. Most have black-color edges and legs, but I've seen some that were trimmed in brown. These brown-color Tables are definitely "factory original", and they appear to be of earlier manufacture.

Please note that the opening in Card Tables was designed for the regular 5-1/2 inch long swinging bed extension on most of the black and the beige-color machines. Therefore, the 221K7 "white" British machine will not fit properly since its bed extension is shorter, at 3-1/2 inches. Another exception is the very earliest black-color *Model 221's* in Series AD and early AE that have a bobbin winder tensioner on the front side of the machine bed. These machines will not fit the opening comfortably.

Card Tables are serial numbered on the underside of the table surface; most have a letter followed by a six digit number. However, some Tables have three digits followed by a letter, or a letter followed by three digits. All of the brown-trimmed Tables I've seen had one of these three digit conventions, and I believe these are of earlier vintage. The Table's serial number is also stamped on its removable piece or cover. This was intended to positively match the cover with its Table. Not a problem for the housewife with one Table at home, but possibly a big one back in the factory or store where multiple Card Tables were being handled. Also, the grain pattern in the veneer is unique to each Table, and there is some slight variation in the physical fit of the covers in their openings.

I haven't extensively researched the serial numbers on Card Tables as I have for *Featherweights*. One of my Card Tables is serial numbered C 114598, and another that's owned by a friend is at the other end of the range - T 100550 - so it would appear they were made in fairly large numbers. However, relatively few of my seven hundred plus letters from machine owners reference a Card Table. They are rarely seen in advertisements or the vendor rows at quilt shows. I believe many of them just wore out from uses other than sewing. Maybe they were too much of an utility table. Most every one I've seen had paint splatters, cooking oil stains, pan burns, etc. on its surface. If you own one, treasure it for the rare *Featherweight* accessory that it is, especially if its veneer and varnish are in good shape.

Early Card Table

There are two versions of the Card Table, both very similar except for some minor design details. The first version is the Model 308, introduced sometime between 1935 and 1938. That's the closest I can get right now. Its removable insert was held in place by a springy piece of flat steel that was manually rotated to lock/unlock by engaging slots in the table frame. There were some subtle changes over time. Many of these Card Tables have a metal trim around the wooden edges, with a metal underframe. But some don't have the metal edge trim. Also, most legs are metal, and others are plain wood. Black is the predominant trim color, but brown was also used. Someone could write a research paper on these Card Tables alone! What did the Model 308 Utility Table cost? I learned from a woman in Wisconsin who inherited her Mother's Card Table and *Featherweight* that they cost $28. and $98., respectively, in May, 1941. She wrote that her parents married on May 1 of that year in Grand Coulee, Washington. . . ."so it must have been the first purchase beyond food and rent".

Believe it or not, an extension was available for the 308 Utility Table - to make, in effect, two connecting tables! The Model 308-1/2 Extension Set was a semi-table with only two legs on its left side. It's attached to the Utility Table opposite the end that holds the machine. It is tailor made for machine quilters, providing even more room for fabric. The Extension Set table had two hooks opposite its legs. To install, it was tilted downward to engage the hooks onto the edge of the Utility Table. Then, the Extension table was raised and its legs were lowered into place. These Extension Set tables were not serial numbered.

Folding Utility Table (Card Table)

Later Card Table

The second version of the Card Table is the Model 312 Utility Table. I'm not sure when it was introduced, but it was advertised along with *Singer's* first slant needle machine, the Model 301, in 1951. The earlier Model 308 Table was indicated as "inactive" at the same time, so they are probably pre-war and post-war versions, respectively. Functionally, it's the same as the earlier Model 308 Table, but its design changed slightly because a different mechanism was used to retain the removable insert. Instead of the flat metal piece that rotated into slots, it used a simple spring clip on one end of the insert and two metal locating tabs at the other end. The removable inserts are not interchangeable between the Model 308 and 312 Utility Tables. This redesign was undoubtedly a cost cutting measure, but it works very well indeed. Serial numbering was the same as before, with the insert being match-numbered to the Table. All of the Model 312 Utility Tables I've owned or have reports on have wooden edges and black-color trim. I have never seen a Model 312 with brown edges and legs.

Dale Pickens and Bob's Picture Box

Utility Table and Extension Set

103

The Model 312 Table sold for $30. in 1960, while the *Featherweight* machine was priced at $149.50. And there was a "special combination price" offer of the machine along with a Model 312 Utility Table at $169.50. And, finally, you guessed it, a Model 312-1/2 Extension Set was available and priced $20. Functionally, the 312-1/2 Extension Set works exactly as described earlier for the 308-1/2 Extension.

I've heard, but not confirmed, that the Extension Set will only work with a matching Table. That is, the semi-table was made for a Card Table with metal trim around the edges, or for a Card Table with plain wooden edges. Buyers of Extension Sets would be well advised to check that the hooks on the semi-table will properly engage the edge of the Utility Table before making the purchase.

Early American Model 68 Cabinet

One of the more exotic Featherweight accessories is the Early American Model 68 Cabinet. When I wrote the first edition of this book I didn't even know they existed. But then I saw one! At first I wasn't sure it was a genuine Singer product, but then I spotted the telltale "Simanco" trademarks. This Cabinet has early American styling and is made especially for the Featherweight. It has an oval top and two swing out front doors, with a rack for extra spools of thread on the inside of the right door. The doors opened to a compartment that is large enough to store the machine when it's not being used. When in use, the oval top is removed and the machine sits in a recess that has metal cross braces and tabs to hold it securely. There's even a built-in wooden box under the top to hold the box of machine attachments. The cabinet is finished in maple.

What I know at present is the Early American Cabinet was introduced in the late 40's and sold into the 1950's. They were listed during Singer's Centennial year in 1951. But at this point I don't know when the Cabinet was discontinued by the factory. Period literature suggests it may have been by about 1955. One woman wrote that she bought one at the local Singer Sewing Center in 1958. But she recalled it might have been "old stock". All told, it appears that the Early American Cabinet was marketed for less than ten years. There are very few examples out there today so it doesn't appear to have been too popular. I'm not sure why. It may be that a fixed piece of fine furniture like the Early American Cabinet was contrary to the concept of a portable sewing machine. A Card Table, yes . . . . but a Cabinet, maybe not. Also, there usually wasn't enough money to buy all the accessories. Let me illustrate this point. I have two copies of a particular *Singer* sales brochure dated July, 1949, in my collection. Curiously, both copies have penciled-in dollar figures, obviously written by women who were shopping for the right combination of heads (machines), cabinets and stools. Both customers priced out a *Featherweight* and a 3-Way Table. The pencil figures are there in both brochures. However, neither woman considered the Model 68 Cabinet! You can form your own conclusions.

The Model 68 Cabinet is not readily identified as a *Singer* product. Nowhere does it say *Singer* or Model 68 or anything that would give you a clue. The closest you'll get is the *Singer* trademark "Simanco" on the bottom of the hardware inside its doors. Oftentimes, people think the Model 68 is just an end table, or possibly a piece of after market sewing furniture. One woman from Ohio related how she got her first *Featherweight*. She began her search and found a Card Table right off. Then she came across

Early American Model 68 Cabinet

Model 68 Cabinet in use

105

two machines at a local dealer. One was from the late 1940's and the second was a 1950's vintage Featherweight that came with a curious oval top cabinet. The man insisted he had gotten the machine and cabinet as a set from their original owner. She couldn't find any identification on the Cabinet, and she bypassed that one and bought the older machine.

What are they worth today? I'm going to say that I really don't know. I've come across a very few of the Model 68 Cabinets in my travels, and none of them were for sale. However, in coming years more examples should come to light as people start looking for the "end table" that fits a Featherweight. And I'm sure some will start changing hands. This will give us something to go by when trying to establish their current value.

Who Made Them?
I've often been asked who made the wooden cabinets, tables, stands and sewing stools for Singer. There's a prevalent feeling that they were manufactured by one or more suppliers. Several people have even written to me in hopes of locating a warehouse with long forgotten Card Tables or even parts. No . . . . the short answer is that Singer made most of them itself. This was dictated by high sales volumes and stringent quality specifications. Wood was used in the pre-plastics days and there was a huge demand for the forest resource. So, Singer had its own sawmill and cabinetwork plant, located in Thurso, Quebec. And, believe it or not, the volume of wood cut-offs and chips was so large that a small Kraft pulp mill was operated on the same site to process what would otherwise be waste.

My husband was traveling on business a few months ago and he was in Ottawa, Ontario. Thurso is located a few miles from there, so he visited the town. Frank talked with residents, former employees, and some folks who work at the present-day pulp mill and sawmill. He learned they were sold by the parent company many years ago, and are now separately owned. Both are doing well, although neither industry is apparently involved in the sewing machine woodwork business at present.

Utility Table Repairs

The Singer Card Tables and their Extension Sets were well designed and built and they've stood up well considering the rigors many were subject to over the years. Other than paint touch-up here and there, only two areas of repair are likely.

The first one is relatively simple. Once the insert is removed, the *Featherweight* presses into spring clips that position and hold it while in the Table. These clips were originally faced with leather or felt to protect the machine from scratching. On many tables, the facings are badly worn or even missing. Repairs can be easily made using leather from a discarded shoe, or felt that can be readily purchased. Most craft glues will do, just be sure to check the label to see if it's good for leather/felt and metal.

The second problem is more serious and it merits long and careful thought. The top of the Card Table or Extension Set may be worn excessively, or its veneer may be delaminating. Now I'm not talking here about a few scratches, wear marks or even burns from hot cooking pans - these are reasonable and should be expected. Remember that the Card Table was designed to serve partial duty as a Utility Table. In this case, no real action is required. You may want to use some good furniture polish to spiffy it up a bit. A worn top is at least original and it speaks volumes from an historical perspective. I'd much prefer to have a scratched or worn top than one that's been refinished or replaced. This is the same advice most antique experts would give to you if you were considering re-doing a piece of period furniture that has significant value and is expected to escalate even higher in years to come.

So, let's say your Card Table had been used to dice vegetables for years, or it's delaminating, or there's a hole punched or burned through it. What to do? If it isn't too bad you can have it refinished. Try to match the original varnish as much as possible. I'd recommend you use a reputable refinisher who knows what she/he's doing. Another option is to replace the veneer. Many species of veneer are available and I'd recommend you go with birch, as was originally used. It's not the cheapest but at least its grain pattern will look original. Again, though, let me stress that these options are only for severe cases of outright Table abuse.

CHAPTER FOURTEEN

COMMON MACHINE PROBLEMS

The *Featherweight Model 221* was designed and built to last, and it does! But every mechanical device wears out sooner or later. Given enough sewing over enough years, and especially if the machine was abused, serious adjustments and repairs will be necessary. These are outside of the scope of this book. Quite frankly, providing directions for something like - how to adjust the timing of the rotary sewing hook - scares me. Most of us have some level of mechanical aptitude, but in many cases we are quick to roll up our sleeves and start taking things apart without truly understanding what the cause of the problem is. In other cases, special tools are needed. Also, small parts are easily lost - they may be difficult or almost impossible to replace. The best advice I can give you is to take your machine to a Singer Service Center for major repairs. Also, there are many skilled tradesmen in smaller shops who have earned their reputations performing these services. The price you pay is well worth the peace of mind knowing the job is done right.

So - this Chapter only deals with the common, minor problems that owners may face after buying and "dusting off" the *Featherweight Model 221* machine you searched for so diligently. All of these may be easily resolved by most anyone.

Setting the Needle
By far, the most common problem when using a *Featherweight* for the first time is the needle is put in wrong. The location of the thumb screw may give the impression it tightens against the flat side of the needle's shank. This is incorrect. Remember that the flat side of the needle's shank must be to the left (toward the swinging bed extension).

Needle Threading
I can't tell you how many times I've helped folks who have a *Featherweight* that won't form a stitch. Usually the solution is simple - incorrect needle threading. The machine's needle must be

threaded <u>from right to left</u>. The majority of newer sewing machines do thread left to right, or front to back, so owners who own or use other machines must remember this peculiarity when operating their *Singer Model 221.*

Sluggish Machine

One of the more common problems is a "slow machine". The machine seems sluggish, or it may not turn over at all. Its drive belt may slip and your first inclination will be to tighten it. Please don't just yet. Or, if the balance wheel does turn over, the machine may feel tight. It just doesn't seem as peppy as it should be. These are warning signs and they're especially common with *Featherweights* that have been idle for long periods of time, maybe years or even decades. Usually this range of problems can be traced back to one or more of four possible causes.

First — Oil Gumming/Dirt

The first scenario is its lubricating oil may have "gummed up", or dirt may have worked into one or more bearings. Your Featherweight has many rotating and sliding parts and all of them move in some kind of bushing, a simple type of bearing. Oil holes or open access areas are there so users can get oil into these bearings. Now, if a previous owner has used anything except the very best sewing machine oil there's a good chance it has oxidized over time. When this happens the oil changes from a light, slippery fluid into a thick, gummy substance. Naturally, it will cause the parts to stick and the machine to run hard. The second possibility is some dirt may have rolled and jammed inside a bearing. Again, this will cause the machine to be sluggish. Short of disassembling of your machine, a solvent must be used to dissolve the gum, or to wash any dirt from bearings.

Since writing the first edition of this book I've tried many solvents, finally settling on refined kerosene (paraffin in the U.K.). The type I buy is clear (so-called "white kerosene") and is practically odorless. Many automobile service stations sell it, and it's marketed mainly for portable heaters to be used in the home. You can also get kerosene in many stores. It's used for wick-type oil lamps. Kerosene has advantages over other materials I've used - it's a superior solvent for petroleum-based oils and lubricants, and it's a light oil itself.

So it provides some lubrication while doing its thing as a solvent. Again, the clear or white type is almost odorless. If your auto service center or store has yellow or lemon-color kerosene, test it for objectionable odor before you buy any. Also, I would not use any color tinted kerosene, i.e., red, blue, etc., as is sold for decorative purposes with oil lamps. Note that you'll only use a very small amount - possibly less than a teaspoon.

Now for a means to get the kerosene into the machine's oil holes and the small nooks and crannies around the sliding parts. If you're not sure where they are, refer to the instructions for oiling that are in the Machine Pamphlet Chapter later in this book. I use a small oil bottle I bought at the local hardware store. It has a tip (about 1/8-inch in diameter) that fits into the oil holes. An oil bottle is easiest but you can improvise with a small straw, like the ones available at the coffee counter at convenience stores. Using a small straw, you put one end into the kerosene, put a finger tip on the other end to seal it, and withdraw, holding the finger tip in place all the while. Then, put the kerosene end into the oil hole and release your finger. The liquid flows exactly where you want it - no muss, no fuss! On a safety note, let me say you should be careful when using kerosene. It's a petroleum product and it is flammable. You shouldn't smoke or have any open flame source around when using it. Keep children away. Also, be careful it doesn't drip and stain your work, or get on the sewing table or carpet.

Here's the procedure for hard running machines. First, unthread your machine. Next, simply inject a small amount of kerosene into all of the bearing and sliding surfaces and let sit for a few minutes. It will start to dissolve any gummy oil and free things up. Then, lift your machine's presser foot up and run for a few minutes - it's important that you don't operate the machine with the presser foot against the feed dog without fabric between them. That's why the presser foot is up. Also, be sure that the stop motion clamp screw in the center of the balance wheel is engaged (tightened clockwise) so the entire mechanism is turning over. Finally, after a few minutes of operation you should stop, wipe off any kerosene, and re-oil the machine using a high quality sewing machine oil such as *Singer's* product. This is important as kerosene doesn't have good lubrication properties for long term use.

For all I know there may be better combo solvents/oils for this application. As I mentioned, I tried many of them on the market. Some were great solvents but they didn't seem to lubricate as well while the machine was running to loosen things up. Others were mainly lubricants, with Teflon or similar wonder ingredients. I wondered about the residue that would be left in the machine bearings. Remember, you only need a good solvent/lubricant for a few minutes of use. Kerosene is excellent for this purpose and that's what I use. Then I apply the sewing machine oil that *Singer* recommends.

Second — Motor Grease

The second possible cause for a sluggish machine is that the motor grease may have thickened up and is causing a drag. This is a common problem with black or beige-color machines that haven't been used regularly. (The 221K7 "white" machine motor doesn't have provisions for greasing.) The older *Featherweights* have the regular *Singer* bracket type motor that's been around for years. This motor has two grease cups or tubes that must be filled periodically, and Singer motor lubricant is the proper grease. *Singer* recommends refilling every 6 to 12 months' of normal use. Do not, under any circumstances, try to inject oil or anything similar into the motor's grease tubes. If you do, the oil will find its way onto the motor commutator or will saturate its brushes - they are made of carbon and must be kept bone dry for proper operation. Also, ordinary grease will not do since it's affected by rising temperature as the motor is working. Problems here are apparent by sluggish operation, motor smoking and overheating.

Eventually, thickened grease frees-up with use but we want to hasten the process. I've been successful using a simple procedure. First, get your portable hair dryer. Next, remove the drive belt from the machine's balance wheel and motor pulley, and run the motor at high speed. While it's whirring away, use the hair dryer at its maximum temperature setting to blow hot air on both ends of the motor. This will help the grease to flow and redistribute itself on the motor bushings. The final step is to refill the grease tubes using fresh Singer motor lubricant. Only squeeze enough grease in each tube to fill it. Incidentally, I've heard that this grease is hard to find in some locations. I bought one in a plastic tube recently under part number 190613. One tube should last anyone a lifetime.

Third — Thread Jamming

Let me tell you about one of the most frustrating problems I ever encountered on a balky machine. But it proved to be an easy one to fix once I figured out what was wrong. In fact, it's more difficult to write about than to resolve. Here's what happened. I had a *Featherweight* that was still tight after trying both procedures described here. I could still feel a lot of drag when I turned its balance wheel by hand. After hours of tedious searching I found that a very small piece of thread had found its way behind the bobbin case and into the rotary hook stitch forming mechanism. This mechanism has a rotating part (called the rotary sewing hook assembly) that revolves around the bobbin case base, which is stationary (doesn't move). Everything has a tight clearance, and the piece of thread was jamming things up. I tried to pull it out with tweezers but it was caught too tightly. So I had to figure out how to disassemble things. It worked! After putting the stitch forming mechanism back together I was pleased to see the machine purr along. Then, right after this experience I had the same problem with another machine I bought. I went ahead and fixed it. And within weeks I helped a woman in a workshop I taught in Chicago. I concluded the thread jamming problem is fairly common, so I included my procedure in the first edition. Since then I've talked with and heard from loads of women who thanked me for this hint. Several commented that it, alone, was worth the price of the book.

The *Model 221* is probably one of the worst machines for tightening or locking up when a thread gets caught in the hook assembly. You may wonder, as I did, why it's so prone to this thread jamming problem. I had a long talk one day with a former *Singer* service man who told me that the machine is just built too well! There are no sloppy clearances or loose fits. So a piece of thread behind the bobbin case base has nowhere to go and can easily bind things up. My directions will help you clear this type of jam. But let's try to prevent it to begin with. Here's a tip I learned from a woman in Texas - her repair man has 30 plus years of experience with *Model 221's*. Although he has nothing but praise for them, he does have one qualifier. Remember to always stop the machine with the thread take up lever in the high position . . . . to keep the thread from tangling in the bobbin area. If the lever is anywhere but up, the mechanism is forming a stitch and the thread can become loose in the rotary hook. I think this is a great idea and I use it all the time. It can be easily accomplished by remembering to turn the handwheel to lift the thread take up lever after you finish your sewing. If you're not sure what this lever is, refer to the illustration at the start of Chapter Four.

I'll give you directions to disassemble and reassemble the most common type of bobbin case base. This is the so-called "latest style" that was supplied with all Featherweights since about 1935. (The very early machines have the "old style" bobbin case base which is much more difficult to access.) So, if you have a post-1935 machine with this problem, here's the procedure. The only tool you'll need is a tiny jeweler's screwdriver. I found one at the local hardware store. It measures two millimeters wide at its tip (about 1/12-inch). To start out, be sure your machine is unplugged. Now, if you flip up your machine's swinging bed extension; you'll be looking at the stitch forming mechanism. Notice how it rotates when you turn the machine's balance wheel by hand. Then . . . .

A) Lift the machine's presser foot.

B) Remove the (two) throat plate screws, then remove the plate by working it under the bed extension with your fingers.

C) Open the bobbin case latch and remove the case.

D) Using your small screwdriver, take out the tiny gib screw shown in illustration 1, be sure to put it where it won't be lost! A small jar is good. Remember that replacement screws are no longer available.

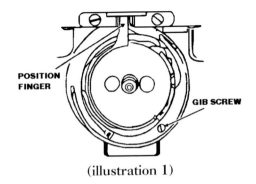

POSITION FINGER

GIB SCREW

(illustration 1)

E) Pivot the retainer (gib) downward as shown in illustration 2. It may be a bit tight but it will move. You can help by putting a wooden toothpick in the hole and pushing outward. <u>Do not</u> use your screwdriver! It may damage the threads the gib screw fits into.

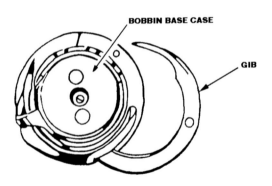

BOBBIN BASE CASE

GIB

(illustration 2)

F) Refer to illustration 3. Rotate the bobbin case base with a finger tip until the point on its edge is just below the point on the sewing hook.

114

G) In this position and this position only the bobbin case base may be removed. Using your finger tips, squeeze the raised edge opposite its "position finger" and pull outward. (Be sure you are pulling on the raised edge, not the stud that sticks out of its center.) You may have to spin it a bit each way to find the exact position. Caution! Do not use pliers! If you want to resort to using pliers, the parts positioning is not correct.

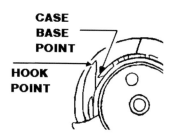

CASE
BASE
POINT

HOOK
POINT

(illustration 3)

H) Check for a stuck thread or heavy lint, etc.

Now, let's put your machine back together. The first thing you want to do is to put a drop of sewing machine oil on the back side of the bobbin case base. This will insure the parts do not run dry after reassembly. Then, follow these instructions.

I) Put the bobbin case base back in the same position as shown in illustration 3. Holding the base by the raised edge opposite its position finger, spin a bit each way until it "seats".

J) Pivot the retainer (gib) upward to the original location. The small hole in the retainer must align with the screw hole below it.

K) Replace the tiny gib screw. Tweezers are good to hold the screw until you start it in place. Don't over tighten!

115

L) Now, rotate the assembled mechanism until the position finger on the bobbin base case is pointing upward (toward the needle). Replace the throat plate by working it back under the swinging bed extension. Be sure the position finger enters the notch of the position plate that's under the throat plate.

M) Replace the (two) throat plate screws, put the bobbin case and bobbin back on and begin sewing.

Fourth — Foot Controller

I discovered another cause for a sluggish machine by accident. And, since then I've found it's fairly common. Despite using all the steps outlined here, one *Featherweight* I bought just wouldn't come up to full speed. It sewed well, but just not fast enough. Turning the balance wheel, it seemed free, nothing was binding. I was perplexed. Then one day I had several machines on the floor showing them to a friend, and I accidentally plugged the foot controller from another machine into the sluggish one. It took off like a scared rabbit!

My husband took the bad foot controller apart, comparing it with one we knew was good. Everything was tight inside but he noticed one part of the mechanism was broken, probably from someone "mashing down" on the pedal. The broken part kept some electrical points on the cross slide from contacting the short-circuiting strips for operation at full speed. He made another part from a piece of copper and I was off and running with that *Featherweight*. Since then, I've seen and heard of similar problems with other foot controllers. Usually their owners are trying to find a replacement unit.

The *Model 221* is designed to operate at a motor speed that's between 900 and 1400 rpm under load. And its foot controller is supposed to start the motor, allow operation anywhere in this range, and stop it when released. The controller has a carbon resistance unit inside to vary the speed of the motor. Three different foot controllers (carbon units) cover the complete range of A.C. and D.C. motors that were available. Compare the identification plates on each part to verify the voltage match.

If your machine's been used a lot, its foot controller/carbon resistance unit may need an adjustment to permit full speed operation. Yes, they can be adjusted! Recently we were at a Quilt Show when a man who serviced sewing machines for years came up and started talking Featherweights. In the course of our talk he explained how to adjust the carbon resistance unit if an otherwise good machine just won't come up to speed. Neither Frank nor I had heard of this possibility before. It was a bit above my level of electrical knowledge but Frank understood the concept. When we came home he looked at three slow controllers and was able to fix two of them. But he tells me it's much too complicated to explain here, even with a diagram or sketch, and especially for would-be electricians who might get hurt.

I mentioned this problem because it's another possibility for repair of a slow machine. If you have one and the previous steps haven't helped, have a qualified service person look at your foot controller. There may be a bent or broken part, or the carbon resistance unit may need an adjustment. Another possibility is the motor armature may be partially burned out - a major problem. More on this later in this chapter. However, if the foot controller can be adjusted you'll avoid the expense of a new one; plus you can maintain the originality of your machine.

Horizontal Arm Shaft "End Play"
One peculiarity of the Featherweight may be experienced after a long stint of heavy sewing. The machine may seem like it's working hard - it may slow down and even bind up. Then, after a rest, it works fine again. I've had this happen to me and I've heard of it from others. And I almost made one Featherweight into a "parts machine" because of it!

This problem happens because its aluminum arm casting expands slightly from working friction and heat from the sewing lamp. This puts end pressure against the hand wheel bushing. Yes, Singer's engineers did recognize this possibility; and the machine was set up to make allowance for heat expansion. Unfortunately, though, a service person may have disturbed it after leaving the factory - setting the arm shaft clearance as is normal for other common models. Such an adjustment will be too tight for the *Model 221*.

117

To avoid having this problem when you really need your machine, check it when the *Featherweight* hasn't been run and is at room temperature. When properly adjusted, you should hear a slight "click" and feel a very small amount of end play when you push-pull on the hand wheel. (The design clearance is only 0.003-inch - about the thickness of a sheet of note paper.) If you hear a click and feel the clearance . . . . great! You're ready to sew up a storm! On the other hand, if your machine is tight when it's cold, it will bind up when it's hot from running. Do-it-yourself adjustment of arm shaft play is not for the average person, thus it's outside the scope of this book. I'd recommend you take your machine to a *Singer* service center for adjustment. It will pay off in the long run, through reduced wear and tear.

Motor Problems

Although motors generally have long service lives, their bushings and brushes do wear, and they do partially or completely burn out. To my knowledge, an exact replacement motor <u>is not available</u> at present for the *Featherweight* machine. Be very careful when buying a Model 221 - try to run it to be sure it will come up to full speed. Also, be sure the motor and foot controller voltages match the household supply where you live. They are labeled. For the U.S. and Canada this is 110 to 120 volts. Machines that are so equipped will also work (with a common step-down transformer) in the U.K. and other countries where the line voltage is nominally 230 volts. They are readily available in catalogs for tourists. It's also possible to use a 230-250 volt machine/foot controller in the U.S. or Canada. In this case, you must get a voltage step-up transformer - they are not as readily available in the U.S. Be sure you know what you're buying!

If your motor is slow or bad, consider having it rebuilt or replaced with a new unit. Yes, there are shops that offer rebuilding service. Cost will be relatively high, especially if the armature must be rewound - but you'll maintain the originality of your machine. Alternately, you can have a currently-manufactured motor installed. One wholesale house offers a changeover kit - with a motor, adapter bracket and belt - for a very nominal cost. Of course, the motor is different than the original version, and I'm told it runs slightly faster than the 1400 rpm (max.) factory motor. Going with a replacement,

118

cost will be somewhat lower than rebuilding and you'll end up with a motor that is factory fresh, although not exactly as supplied by *Singer*. Most sewing machine repair shops can secure the parts from their wholesalers and make the swap.

Position Finger Location

Not infrequently, one will buy a *Featherweight* that just won't form a stitch. The machine appears to be okay otherwise; and you've already checked for proper needle installation and threading. Sadly, it seems that many women had put away their machines because of this problem, usually after doing nothing more than removing the throat plate for cleaning. One woman told me she had somehow "messed things up" while doing a routine cleaning of lint. Afterwards she'd retired her machine because the repair shop was miles away in the next county. For perspective, about ten percent of the machines that passed through my hands have had this problem. I've gotten so that it's one of the first things I check when looking at a machine that's offered for sale. Particularly at a lawn sale or flea market where electricity isn't available to run and sew with the machine.

Fortunately, this is an easy mystery to resolve. You'll want to check out the location of the position finger on the bobbin case base. It must be <u>pointed up</u> and "captured" in the notch under the throat plate. Flip up the Featherweight's swinging bed extension and refer to the following illustration:

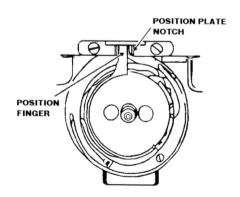

It is very, very important that the position finger on the bobbin case base enters the notch of the "position plate" that's located on the underside of the throat plate. Otherwise, the machine won't form a stitch. If yours isn't in the notch, remove the throat plate (two screws), turn the bobbin case base until its position finger is up, and reinstall the throat plate taking care that notch captures the finger. Also, remember to do this whenever you remove the throat plate to clean lint, etc.

Needle Thread Tensioner

Your Featherweight should be able to form a good "lock stitch", i.e., the threads should meet and lock in the center of the fabric. As all seamstresses know, the upper and lower tensions must be balanced to produce this perfect stitch. The lower thread (on the bobbin) seldom requires a change, so it's the upper (needle) thread that is designed for easy adjustment to create the balance.

Despite moving the needle thread tensioner through its full range, you may not be able to achieve the proper lock stitch. If so, it could be that the tension assembly had been taken apart by a previous owner, and was reassembled incorrectly. A symptom of this on Featherweights is that the tension dial can't be turned through its full range from number 0 (zero) through number 9. (Owners of early Featherweights without numbered needle tension dials can't use this hint). Also, your needle may bend or break when trying to pull thread from the spool - even when the tensioner is at its lightest setting, the machine is properly threaded, and its presser foot is up.

Let me caution readers to avoid taking your tensioner apart if you're not having problems with needle tension or proper lock stitching. Whenever it's disassembled, the factory adjustment for minimum tension will be lost and you'll have to spend time re-locating it. This is unnecessary effort and it can be difficult for some people. On the other hand, if it's already been reassembled incorrectly by a former owner, you have no choice but to go ahead.

Needle Thread Tensioner

Mowry photo

Start by pressing in on the numbered dial (using two finger tips) and unscrewing the thumb nut. Inspect everything for broken or missing parts. Then reassemble, insuring the parts are oriented as shown in the illustration and the description in the next paragraph. You will have to <u>evenly</u> press in on the numbered dial (to overcome the tension spring pressure) to screw the thumb nut fully in place. I usually get a friend to help with this. Two small wooden sticks are good for holding it inward while the thumb nut is screwed in.

Refer to the illustration that follows - it shows the proper arrangement of parts. Note that the tension spring's "tail" fits in the slot on the stud, with its first half-coil <u>facing down</u>. Also, the little tang or projection on the stop washer <u>must be facing up</u>. In other words, the little tang fits into the space above the half-coil on the tension spring. With this positioning, the assembly will adjust needle tension smoothly between the extremes of 0 and 9 on the dial settings.

NEEDLE THREAD TENSION

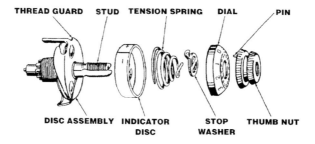

(illustration - Needle tension assembly)

121

Next, to re-locate the proper settings you will adjust the relative positions of the thumb nut and dial, so that zero (0) = minimum tension. Referring to the illustration, you'll see there's a small pin on the back side of the thumb nut. Also, there are many small holes around the face of the dial. This pin can fit into any one of these holes; you must find the <u>one and only</u> hole that is correct. Using your small wooden sticks, press in on the numbered dial to release the pin, then turn the thumb nut to the left (counter clockwise) and engage the next hole. Release the sticks and try pulling thread through the tensioner. If there is some tension, repeat the procedure again and again until you can't feel any tension on the thread. Then, set the thumb nut one hole to the right (clockwise) to produce minimum tension at zero (0) setting on the dial. You are now back to the factory needle thread tensioner setting!

Other Tension Problems

Stitching problems can be usually tracked back to improper machine threading, needle setting, a defective or bent needle, or improper upper/lower tension adjustments. At times, two or more of these will occur simultaneously; and such combinations can tax your troubleshooting skills. In reality, though, it's really a process of studying the problem and eliminating probable causes. Refer to the information presented earlier in this chapter; also to the machine pamphlet reprint section that's later in this book. Now, I'd like to share some information on needle tension myths.

Felt "Washer"

I've heard one interesting (tension problem) story from time to time in my travels. For background, let me share that you may have a little felt "washer" on the spool pin of your machine. (The pin is the part the spool of thread fits onto.) I've seen these felt washers in red, green and black. As the story goes, *Singer* supplied this washer in recent years because modern spools of thread are made of plastic, thus are lighter than the earlier wooden spools. This, in turn, is supposed to cause upper thread tension problems - presumably because the plastic spools are too light and easily turned when the machine is running. I've heard that the felt is supposed to increase friction. So . . . . elusive tension problems are often blamed on the lack of this magic felt washer.

I find this story amusing because I have a 1935-dated manual for the Featherweight that shows a felt washer proudly in place on a *Model 221*. This was long before plastic spools came into use. The felt washer is part # 170441 and it's properly called the arm spool pin washer. Also, the very same part is the proper felt washer use under the thumb nut that holds the bed cover plate (beneath the machine) in place. Here it acts as an oil and grease seal. So why did Singer use the red felt washer on the spool pin since about day one of the *Featherweight* ? Simply, it will keep paint from wearing out beneath the rotating spool of thread, especially on machines that are used a lot. So, if you have thread tension problems, please look elsewhere. There isn't any magic in the felt!

Spool Pin Spring

Folks are often curious about the small coil spring that may be found on your machine's spool pin. Again, tension problems are sometimes attributed to its absence. Let me say for the record that this coil spring is a factory item - it's part # 045826 for all machines except the 221K7 "white" British *Featherweight*. And the spring is # 090940 for the 221K7. (The spool pin on the K7 machine is about 1/4-inch shorter than the others, thus its spring is shorter). At this writing they are still available. This spring is intended to go inside the spool of thread, keeping it from spinning too freely when the machine is running. It also keeps the needle thread taut when it is idle, or if the spool is left in place when the machine is stored or moved. It has almost nothing to do with tension problems. I said "almost" because the needle thread tensioner has more than enough range of adjustment to compensate for its presence or absence inside the thread spool. That is, slightly less tension may be necessary if you have a spring on the spool pin. I like to have them on my *Featherweights* because the upper thread doesn't loosen and tangle when I put the machine away. But they're not necessary to be able to achieve proper thread tension balancing.

Machine "Feet"

Let's talk about the little rubber washers that are beneath the four corners of your machine. Most folks call them "feet", although the official names are Bed Cushion and Base Cushion - both are used. The feet or cushions are designed to keep the machine level when sewing, and to protect your table from scratches. Oftentimes, one or more are missing, or you may find the rubber has started to deteriorate. I've seen many that were gummy and sticky.

In the first edition of this book I wrote about using a certain size flat neoprene faucet washer as a replacement. Since then I've heard about using such things as pop bottle caps and rubber bumpers that were ground down to fit. I even received a sketch of a holder for grinding washers that was made from a wooden dowel. My husband looked into having a small run of the proper size feet made up. He even found a manufacturer to do it. And then, wonder of wonders, I discovered they were available from *Singer* - and still are as this is written. The part is # 045780 for the Bed Cushion that's used on 221, black 221K variants, and the 222K Free Arm machines. (Note that five cushions are used on the 222K). You may also want the special retaining screws (part # 050116) which sometimes wear so badly they are hard to remove. Also, part # 148062 is proper for the Base Cushions used on the "white" British 221K7 machines. They are slightly smaller in diameter and are pressed into place, so attachment screws are not needed. Please be sure to order the proper feet for your machine. Cost for either type is very nominal.

CHAPTER FIFTEEN

MACHINE COSMETICS

In this chapter I'm going to address machine cosmetics; I suppose I could use the word "detailing" here. There are a few detail sort of things you should consider to improve the appearance of your classic *Featherweight*. These are touches you can do yourself. But let me start out with an extreme example of what not to do! Someone wrote a while back for my opinion on having a machine repainted at the local auto body repair shop. My advice: don't do it, no matter how badly the machine is worn! Similarly with the gold decals on the machine bed and swinging extension (black-color machine). They may be scratched or worn, but please resist the temptation to scrape them off or dissolve the glue with some sort of solvent. Please remember you own a classic machine that has significant value now, and is likely to escalate even higher in years to come. But it must be "original" to command such values.

Let me also say that a <u>professional</u> refurbishing is a bit different. I have mixed feelings in this regard. Here you have someone who knows what they're doing go ahead to repaint and re-decal the machine. And the machine will look like new except to a very careful observer. But the professional identifies the machine as a rework so a potential customer isn't deceived and history isn't falsified. I can live with this for cases of extreme machine abuse.

Paint Touch-up

Personally, I'd prefer to see a *Featherweight* with the dings and scratches it earned over the years. To my eye, it just looks right that way. However I've seen some machines that have really bad surface chipping. One I bought worked perfectly but it looked like someone had beat on it with a rock. Since a factory refinishing service isn't available, I set out to find a good touch-up paint for this "worst case". And after a bit of work, I found one that worked pretty well. Please recognize, though, that no touch up paint is going to color match exactly, nor will it fill deep dings or chips so they're even with the surface.

My recommendation for the common black-color machine is the high gloss black touch-up paint sold in General Motors dealerships. The one I use is part #12345495, Group 8.800. The exact color is: Black - Code 41/44 - WACC9588. It comes in a small container with a built-in mechanical agitator and an applicator brush. Just be sure to try it on an inconspicuous part of the machine first to see if you'll be happy with the effect.

Touch-up paint for the beige, "green" and bisque *Featherweights* is up to you. The latter two variants have various color tints so it would be well to take your machine to an automobile parts supply store to match with available colors of high gloss paint. Note that you'll want liquid touch-up paint, not spray paint! The beige-color of 221J/J6 machines is at least uniform from machine to machine, but as yet I haven't tried to research a good color match. I guess I'm happy with my J model machines "as is".

Machine Waxing
Several folks have written to tell about spray products they use to keep the machine paint shiny looking. I'm reluctant to mention them here because I'm not sure what their long-term effects will be on the *Featherweight's* paint and/or the gold decals on black-color 221's. Yes, the machine may look good now, but how about five or ten years from now? Whenever I think about this I remember a dining room table we once owned. I bought it from a highly respected retailer and it was a quality table. The ends were varnished wood, real wood, not veneer over a pressed composition of wood chips and glue. But over a period of a few short years their upper varnished surfaces became gummy and sticky (the lowers were okay). They never went back to a hard surface finish. Why? I don't know for sure. Probably due to a reaction with some furniture polish I used. Now, I don't want something like this to happen to my *Model 221's*.

Let me tell you what my husband does with my machines. He uses a premium carnauba car wax. This is the type auto enthusiasts use on the very finest and expensive automobiles. There are several brands on the market. If you decide to do the same, be absolutely sure you buy a non-abrasive type. This is only a wax, not a combination cleaner/wax. The latter will tend to rub through the paint and gold decals. He applies one coat and leaves it at that.

Face Plate Polishing

The last cosmetic touch I'll mention is polishing of the plated face plates on the black-color Featherweights. Occasionally you'll see one that has some surface tarnishing. It may have a yellowish or brownish cast. Here I simply use a household cleaner made for fine table service ware. Just apply according to the directions on its container. I'd recommend you do not use steel wool or the synthetic wool stripping pads that are common today. They work well for their intended purposes, but are too rough for the shiny surface of the plating.

CHAPTER SIXTEEN

PARTS & ACCESSORIES

As interest in *Featherweights* has skyrocketed over recent years, so too has the demand for replacement parts and accessories. It's a well designed and built sewing machine; most of them sew and sew for generations with nothing but a worn-out belt or two. But any mechanical device can and will wear out. And parts will be lost or broken from misfortune and abuse. Fortunately, many parts are still available from Singer. But others are not.

A commonly asked for part is the bobbin case - part # 045751. It's easily misplaced or lost. Fortunately it's still available from the factory. This bobbin case will fit all 221 and 222 *Featherweight* machines, also their big sister - the Model 301 slant needle machine. So . . . . factory and after market parts supply should be assured for years to come. Similarly with the

Singer® Model 301 Slant Needle Machine

Barb and Les Perrin

bobbin case base. Here, the part is held in place on the machine so it doesn't become lost. Nor does it wear out. Breakage, due mainly to improper disassembly, accounts for most if not all of the problems with it. At this writing it's also available - part # 045926. And, if you need the entire rotary hook assembly you can still order one under part # 045924, at a retail list that (hold on to your hats) was a bit over three hundred dollars in the 1995 parts catalog! I'm told that Singer no longer manufactures these parts but gets them from a supplier overseas. So their prices undoubtedly reflect being made in small production runs.

Swinging now to motors, let me repeat earlier information that exact replacement motors are not currently available. Hopefully they will be in the future. I've written about motor problems and repair/replacement options in Chapter 14. Please refer there for guidance if you think your 221's motor is bad.

The last category of parts are those unusual ones that are just not available from recognized sources at any price. In these cases a diligent search for shops and people that have "parts machines" is the only option. Some searches can be easy, and others exhaustive. For instance, one day I chanced into a woman at a quilt class I taught at the Belle Grove Plantation Show in Virginia. She needed a black-color arm cap cover - the part with the pin that holds the spool of thread. Guess what? A man with a parts machine had just called me days earlier. That was an easy one. I gave her his name and number. Then, just recently I had a woman from Canada write to me about her 222K *Featherweight Convertible* Free Arm machine. It had the entire light fixture missing (it's the type with the switch on the right end of the light socket, not on the machine bed). She had searched around in Ontario and had even written to the U.K. to find a replacement. Still no luck when we last corresponded! The Internet, sewing machine repair shops, magazine advertisements, and Quilt Guild networks are all good sources for these unusual parts. But searching can take an inordinate amount of time and effort. I, myself, have had to discontinue doing it for others due to the demands of my traveling and writing schedules.

Fortunately, the *Featherweight* Accessory scene is ramping up! More and more original type accessories are appearing for these wonderful sewing machines. At present you can buy a replacement carrying case that very closely matches the design of the Type Three black carrying case. (This is the one with the compartment on the left side). Pricing is very attractive. You'll see them in advertisements in the quilting magazines and in the vendor rows at major quilt shows. And yes, reproduction Card Tables are even available! The ones I've seen are quite true to the original design of the Model 312, and are reasonably priced. Again, I've seen them in magazine adverts and at shows. My prediction is we'll see more and more accessories appearing as time goes on. Where there's a pressing need, some entrepreneur will step forward to fill it!

CHAPTER SEVENTEEN

THE FUTURE

I t's hard to believe some of the *Featherweights* purring away in sewing rooms and class are now old enough to qualify for social security, but there they are - proud of their Depression era birthdates and not only alive, but thriving. And they look as modern today as when *Singer* shipped them from its Edison, New Jersey, factory to a cautious public ready for the 1933 World's Fair. As modern and healthy as ever. The *Featherweight's* popularity dimmed a few years back, but it never went away. And now, it seems to have come back stronger than before.

The *Featherweight* will probably never be reproduced as we know it. Even with today's advanced technology - investment casting of parts, and CNC (Computer Numeric Control) machining operations - the design and hand fitting involved in assembling this intricate, finely-crafted portable sewing machine would likely boost its unit cost too highly. This reality just reinforces its status as a classic; an example of craftsmanship that's fast disappearing in this modern world of plastics and throw-aways. This alone makes the *Model 221* well worth owning whether you are a quilter, seamstress, or a collector of fine things that will probably be no more.

CHAPTER EIGHTEEN

LOOKING BACK

This completes my book on the *Singer Featherweight 221* - The Perfect Portable. Whenever I look at one, either one of mine or one in class, I can't help but muse about the places it's been, the things it's seen, and our changing times.

The hard times of the thirties are no more. Many of the women who lived then are gone, their sewing long forgotten except for the few pieces of work carefully stored away in trunks or bureau drawers. Most of the machines they bought on payments with grocery money and cookie jar savings are still around, and many of them are still used and respected as the piece of Americana that they are.

Quiltmaking and sewing have resurged from a dormancy for much of the mid century and have come back like an avalanche. And the *Singer Featherweight 221* goes on. Today, available machines are eagerly fought over by quilters, dealers, repair shops and collectors. Sadly, there are no new sewing machines with the same features as the legendary Model 221. If you're fortunate you already own one. If not, you may consider looking for one.

You'll find them in attics and garages, but mostly in sewing rooms and quilt shops and seminars. I see them often in class, performing flawlessly next to the latest computer controlled wonder. Usually, I sense an element of pride that favors the old *Model 221* over its expensive neighbor. Most of them are scratched and worn around the edges, but their owners don't seem to mind a bit. Some of them are for sale, but many aren't. Ask the woman with a cased *Featherweight* in her hand. She'll probably just shake her head and smile. Perhaps she'll show you a wallet photo of her daughter or granddaughter. Or maybe she'll tell you about her mother or aunt. That *Featherweight* won't be for sale at anything less than a Queen's ransom. Not as long as there are mothers and daughters, women's arts, and an appreciation for things made by patient and skillful human hands. Mine, I know, will be in our family for another generation or two. One is already waiting for our new granddaughter, Casey!

CHAPTER NINETEEN

MACHINE PAMPHLET AND ATTACHMENT INSTRUCTIONS

*S*inger Featherweight machine pamphlets are harder to find than the machines themselves! Usually this booklet is missing from the carrying case, or it may be in poor shape from years of use. I've seen many that were saturated with sewing machine oil. Years ago, one student showed me her *Featherweight* booklet, which was printed in Spanish. Unfortunately, she didn't speak the language - but it was the only one she could find. At least the photos and illustrations were useful.

To help meet this need, I included a partial reprint of this desirable *Singer* booklet, in the first edition of this book. Space limitations allowed me to present most of the pages on the machine itself. Since then I've been asked by many people to include the pages on the machine attachments if I ever updated this book. I'm happy to be able to do it now. The pamphlet I used is a U.S. version dated 1947, about mid-range in the life span of the Model 221 machine. Readers should note that the entire machine pamphlet is not reprinted. Again, book design considerations caused me to bypass some of the general and less critical information in this revised edition.

INSTRUCTIONS

FOR USING

SINGER*

PORTABLE ELECTRIC

SEWING MACHINE

221-1

ROTARY HOOK, FOR FAMILY USE

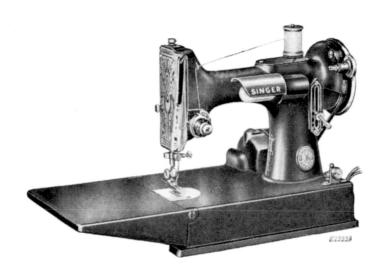

* Reg. U. S. Pat. Off. by

THE SINGER MANUFACTURING COMPANY

SINGERLIGHT

To turn the SINGERLIGHT "on" or "off," a switch is conveniently located at the front of the machine as shown at D, Fig. 7.

To Remove and Replace the Bulb

Do not attempt to unscrew the bulb. It is of the bayonet and socket type and does not unscrew.

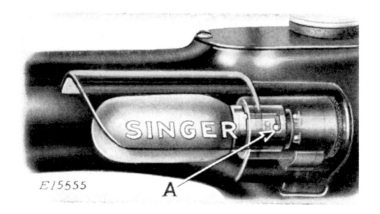

FIG. 3. REPLACING THE BULB

To remove the bulb. Press the bulb into the socket and at the same time turn the bulb over from you as far as it will go, then withdraw the bulb.

To insert a new bulb. Press the bulb into the socket and turn it over toward you until the bulb pin (A) enters the notch in the socket, as shown in Fig. 3.

To Operate the Machine

Raise the presser foot (B) by means of the presser bar lifter (C) to prevent injury to the foot (B) and feed (A).

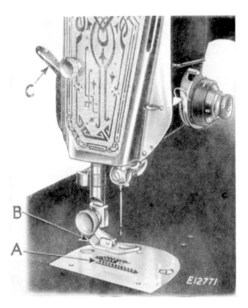

FIG. 5. FRONT VIEW OF THE MACHINE

Place a piece of cloth under the presser foot and let the foot down upon it.

Turn on the electric current and press the foot controller. As the pressure on the foot controller is increased, the speed of the machine is increased, the speed being controlled by the amount of pressure on the foot controller. Operate the machine in this way, without being threaded, until you have become accustomed to guiding the material and operating the foot controller.

To Remove the Bobbin

Turn the balance wheel over toward you until the thread take-up lever (6, Fig. 13) is raised to

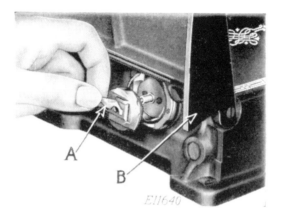

FIG. 6. REMOVING THE BOBBIN CASE

its highest position. Raise the bed extension (B, Fig. 6) as far as it will go and with the thumb and forefinger of the left hand open the bobbin case latch (A, Fig. 6) and lift out the bobbin case. While the latch remains open, the bobbin is retained in the bobbin case. Release the latch, turn the open end of the bobbin case downward and the bobbin will drop out.

To Wind the Bobbin

It is necessary to understand the stop motion (B, Fig. 7) by which the balance wheel (A, Fig. 7) can be released when required, thus permitting the winding of bobbins without running the stitching mechanism.

Release the balance wheel by turning the stop motion screw (B, Fig. 7) over toward you. It is necessary to hold the balance wheel while loosening the stop motion screw.

Place the bobbin on the bobbin winder spindle
and push it on as far as it will go. Put the spool of

Fig. 7. Winding the Bobbin

thread on the spool pin (1) and pass the thread from
the spool into the thread guide (2), then under and
between the tension discs (3) at the front of the bed
and through one of the holes in the left side of the
bobbin (4) from the inside. Press down the bobbin
winder pulley against the belt. Then press the foot
controller the same as for sewing.

The end of the thread must be held by hand
until a few coils are wound and should then be
broken off. When sufficient thread has been wound
upon the bobbin, pull the bobbin winder pulley away
from the belt and remove the bobbin from the
spindle.

If the thread does not wind evenly on the bobbin,
loosen the screw which holds the tension bracket
(3) in position on the bed of the machine and slide
the tension bracket to the right or left, as may be
required, then tighten the screw.

138

To Thread the Bobbin Case

Hold the bobbin between the thumb and forefinger of the right hand, with the thread on top drawing from right to left, as shown in Fig. 8.

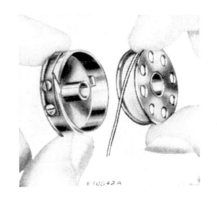

FIG. 8

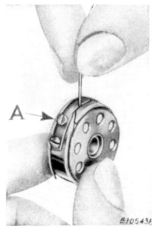

FIG. 9

Then pull the thread into the slot as shown in Fig. 9, and back under the tension spring into the slot at the end of the tension spring as shown in Fig. 10.

With the left hand hold the bobbin case as shown in Fig. 8, the slot in the edge being at the top, and place the bobbin into the bobbin case.

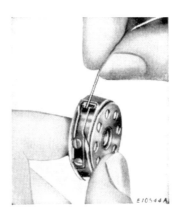

FIG. 10

To Replace the Bobbin Case

After threading, take the bobbin case by the latch, holding it between the thumb and forefinger

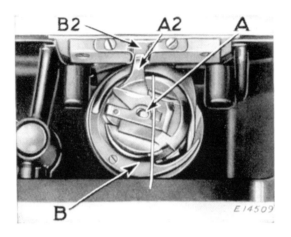

FIG. 11. BOBBIN CASE THREADED AND REPLACED

of the left hand. Place the bobbin case on the center stud (A, Fig. 11) of the bobbin case base with the thread drawing from the top of the bobbin case. Release the latch and press the bobbin case back until the latch catches the groove near the end of the stud. Allow about three inches of thread to hang free from the bobbin case and turn down the bed extension.

CAUTION—In case the throat plate is removed for cleaning the stitch-forming mechanism, etc., **make certain,** when replacing the throat plate, that the position finger (A2, Fig. 11) of the bobbin case base enters the notch (B2, Fig. 11) of the position plate attached to the underside of the throat plate.

To Set the Needle

Turn the balance wheel over toward you until the needle bar is at its highest position, and loosen the thumb screw (A, Fig. 12) in the needle clamp.

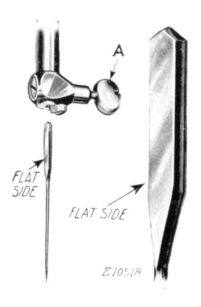

FIG. 12. POSITIONING OF NEEDLE
IN NEEDLE CLAMP

Have the flat side of the shank of the needle toward the left as shown above and put the needle up into the clamp as far as it will go. Then tighten the thumb screw.

To select the correct needle, see inside cover at back of book.

Upper Threading

Turn the balance wheel over toward you until the thread take-up lever (6) is raised to its highest position. Place the spool of thread on the spool pin at the top of the machine; pass the thread into the thread guide (1) at the left, down, under and from right to left between the tension discs (2). Hold the spool tightly with the right hand and with the left hand pull the thread up under the thread take-up spring (4) until it enters the retaining fork (3), then pass the thread up and back of the wire thread guide (5) and from right to left through the hole (6) in the end of the thread take-up lever, down into the eyelet (7), at the side of the face plate, into the lower wire thread guide (8), into the guide (9) in the needle clamp, then from right to left through the eye of the needle (10). Draw about two inches of thread through the eye of the needle with which to commence sewing.

FIG. 13. UPPER THREADING

To Prepare for Sewing

With the left hand hold the end of the thread, leaving it slack from the hand to the needle. Turn

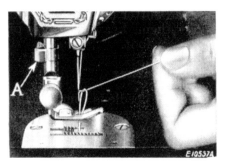

FIG. 14. DRAWING UP BOBBIN THREAD

the balance wheel over toward you until the needle moves down and up again to its highest point, thus catching the bobbin thread. Draw up the needle thread and the bobbin thread will come up with it through the hole in the throat plate, as shown in Fig. 14. Lay both threads back under the presser foot diagonally across the feed, as shown in Fig. 14A, to the right or left, depending upon which side of the needle the material is to be located, so that when the presser foot is lowered, the threads will be firmly held between the feed and the presser foot

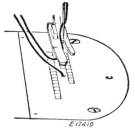

FIG. 14A. THREADS IN POSITION TO COMMENCE SEWING

To Commence Sewing

Place the material beneath the presser foot, lower the presser foot and commence to sew

When sewing thick material, it may be necessary to turn the balance wheel over toward you to start the machine. This should also be done if the machine stops when sewing across thick seams

143

To Remove the Work

Stop the machine with the thread take-up lever (6, Fig 13) at its highest position, raise the presser foot and draw the fabric back and to the left, pass the threads over the thread cutter (A, Fig. 14) and pull down lightly to sever them. Leave the ends of the threads under the presser foot.

To Turn a Corner

Stop the machine when the needle is commencing its upward stroke. Raise the presser foot and turn the work as desired, using the needle as a pivot, then lower the presser foot.

To Regulate the Pressure on the Material

For ordinary family sewing, it is seldom necessary to change the pressure on the material. If sewing fine silk or flimsy material, lighten the pressure by turning the thumb screw (C, Fig. 25) on the top of the machine over to the left so that it screws up. To increase the pressure, turn this thumb screw over to the right so that it screws down. The pressure should be only heavy enough to prevent the material from rising with the needle and to enable the feed to move the work along evenly. The heavier the material, the heavier the pressure; the lighter the material, the lighter the pressure.

To Regulate the Direction of Feed

To feed the goods **from you,** push down the stitch regulator lever (C, Fig. 15) as far as it will go.

To feed the goods **toward you,** raise the stitch regulator (C) as high as it will go.

The direction of the feed can be reversed at any point of a seam without removing the work from the machine.

Back tacking is therefore readily accomplished and the fastening of the ends of seams is made easy.

To Regulate the Length of Stitch

The machine can be adjusted to make from 6 to 30 stitches to the inch, as indicated by the numerals on the stitch indicator plate (A, Fig. 15).

FIG. 15. SHOWING LEVER FOR REVERSING DIRECTION OF FEED AND REGULATING LENGTH OF STITCH

The number of stitches to the inch that the machine is set to make is indicated by the number which is in line with the stitch regulator lever (C, Fig. 15).

To change the length of stitch, screw the thumb nut (B, Fig. 15) away from the stitch indicator plate (A) as far as it will go. Then move the stitch regulator lever (C) until it is in line with the number designating the desired length of stitch and screw the thumb nut (B) inward until it touches the stitch indicator plate.

The machine will now make the indicated number of stitches to the inch in either a forward or reverse direction, depending on whether the lever (C) is at its lowest or highest position.

Basting

The longest stitch made by the machine, No. 6 on the stitch indicator, is found satisfactory for basting, after loosening the tension on the needle thread so that the stitches may be easily pulled from the material.

Machine basting is firmer and more even than that done by hand in addition to being much quicker.

To Sew Flannel or Bias Seams

Use a short stitch and as light a tension as possible on the needle thread so as to leave the thread loose enough in the seam to allow the goods to stretch if necessary.

Tensions

For ordinary stitching, the needle and bobbin threads should be locked in the center of the thickness of the material, thus:

FIG. 16. PERFECT STITCH

If the tension on the needle thread is too tight, or if that on the bobbin thread is too loose, the needle thread will lie straight along the upper surface of the material, thus:

FIG. 17. TIGHT NEEDLE THREAD TENSION

If the tension on the bobbin thread is too tight, or if that on the needle thread is too loose, the bobbin thread will lie straight along the under side of the material, thus:

FIG. 18. LOOSE NEEDLE THREAD TENSION

CAUTION—It is important for the tension thumb nut (B, Fig. 19) to have a firm fit on tension stud (O, Fig. 20, page 20) to keep the numbered dial (D) in the position set for the required tension. To remedy a loose fit of the nut, remove parts B, D, E, F and G, Fig. 20, and slightly spread the stud, then re-assemble the parts as instructed on pages 20 to 23 inclusive.

To Regulate the Needle Thread Tension

The tension on the needle thread can be regulated only when the presser foot is down.

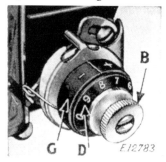

The numbered dial (D, Fig. 19) is marked with arbitrary numbers ranging from 0 to 9 which indicate different degrees of tension that can be produced. The numbers do not denote a particular size of thread. By noting the number which is opposite the center line between the plus and minus signs, on the indicator (G) when set for a satisfactory tension on the work being stitched, the number can be readily reverted to when a change is made in the tension or size of thread.

To increase the tension, turn the thumb nut (B) over to the right until the desired number on the numbered dial (D) is opposite the center line, the highest numbers denoting increased tension.

To decrease the tension, turn the thumb nut (B) over to the left, the lower numbers indicating less tension.

The tension indicator (G) is marked with the signs + and —, which also indicate the direction in which to turn the thumb nut (B) for more or less tension.

To Regulate the Bobbin Thread Tension

The tension on the bobbin thread is regulated by the screw (A, Fig. 9) which is nearest the center of the tension spring on the outside of the bobbin case. To increase the tension, turn the screw (A) over to the right. To decrease the tension, turn this screw over to the left.

When the tension on the bobbin thread has been once properly adjusted, it is seldom necessary to change it, as a correct stitch can usually be obtained by varying the tension on the needle thread.

To Disassemble the Needle Thread Tension

Turn the thumb nut (B, Fig. 20) to the left until it stops at "0" on the numbered dial, then press in

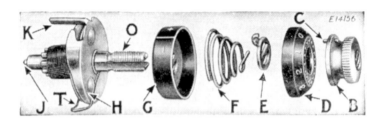

Fig. 20

the dial to disengage the pin (C) in the thumb nut from the dial, and remove the thumb nut and dial, stop washer (E), tension spring (F), indicator (G) and tension disc assembly (H) which includes the thread take-up spring, thread guard plate and two discs.

Note. It is not necessary to remove the stud (O, Fig. 20) from the machine arm in order to disassemble the thread tension. It is shown removed, in Fig. 20, only for the purpose of illustration.

To Reassemble the Needle Thread Tension

First make sure that the tension releasing pin (J), only the end of which is shown in Fig. 20, is in place in the stud (O).

Place the two tension discs (L, Fig. 21) with the flat thread-bearing sides of the discs together in position on the thread guard (M). Then pass the eyelet

148

(N) of the thread take-up spring under the thread guard, having the coils of the spring above the tension discs as shown in Fig. 21.

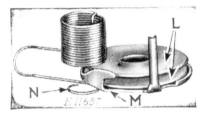

Fig. 21

Guide the tension disc assembly onto the stud so that the extension (K, Fig. 20) of the thread guard enters the hole in the machine arm, and the tail (inside the coil) of the thread take-up spring enters one of the grooves in the stud. Next replace the indicator with the large open side facing the end of

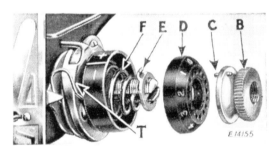

Fig. 22

the stud so that the plus and minus marks will be at the top (with the minus sign at the left) and hold the parts, thus assembled, against the shoulder of the stud. Then insert the tension spring (F, Fig. 20) in the indicator with the first (half) coil of the spring straddling the lower half of the stud. Guide the stop washer (E) onto the stud so that the extension will be above the tension stud. If the spring and stop washer are in correct position, the extension (S) will clear the first (half) coil of the tension spring as shown in Fig. 23.

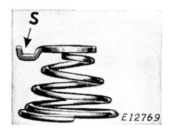

FIG. 23

Next place the numbered dial on the stud so that the numeral 2 is opposite the stop washer extension, then push the dial to compress the spring so that the thumb nut can be turned onto the stud, carefully guiding the pin in the thumb nut into one of the holes of the numbered dial. Then lower the presser bar and turn the thumb nut (B) to the left until it stops at "0." Thread the tension and pull the thread through the tension discs to test the amount of tension on the thread at the "0" position. At this point there should be a slight pull on the thread to indicate that there is a minimum tension, which gradually increases with the turn of the thumb nut to the right, providing a full range of tensions from light to heavy within one revolution of the thumb nut.

If the pull is too strong for a minimum tension, press in the numbered dial to disengage the pin in the thumb nut from the dial, and reset the pin in one of the holes to the **left** of the previous setting. This resetting of the pin will produce less tension at zero. Repeat this process until the minimum desired tension is obtained.

On the other hand, should there be no tension at zero press in the dial and reset the pin in one of the holes to the **right** of the previous setting, repeating this process until a slight minimum tension is obtained.

The tension on the thread take-up spring (T, Fig. 22) should be just sufficient to take up the slack of the needle thread until the eye of the needle reaches the goods in its descent.

If the tension on the thread take-up spring requires adjustment, remove the tension disc assembly, disengage the end of the spring from the groove in the tension stud, revolve the spring and place its end in the groove which produces the correct tension.

If Correct Stitching is Not Obtained:

If the bobbin thread tension has been disturbed, or a correct stitch cannot be obtained without a very heavy or very light needle thread tension, then the following procedure is recommended:

Using No. 50 thread in the needle and on the bobbin, adjust the needle thread tension as instructed above and on page 22. Then turn the tension thumb nut to "3" and, with two thicknesses of thin material in the machine, adjust the bobbin thread tension, as instructed on page 19, until the stitch is correctly locked in the material as shown in Fig. 16.

A wide range of materials and threads can now be accommodated without further adjustment of the bobbin thread tension.

To Oil the Machine

To insure easy running, the machine requires oiling and if used continuously it should be oiled each day. With moderate use, an occasional oiling

FIG. 24. REAR VIEW, SHOWING OILING POINTS

is sufficient. Oil should be applied at each of the places shown by unlettered arrows in Figs. 24, 25 and 26. One drop of oil at each point is sufficient. Oil holes are provided in the machine for bearings which cannot be directly reached.

Turn back the cover at the back of the machine and oil the moving parts inside the arm as indicated in Fig. 24, and occasionally apply a small quantity of **SINGER** MOTOR LUBRICANT to the teeth of the gear (A, Fig. 24), then replace the cover.

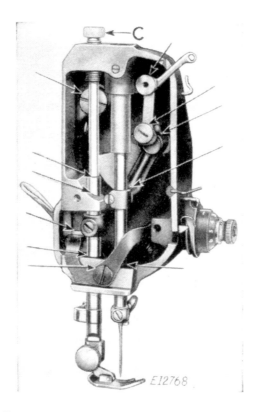

FIG. 25. END VIEW, SHOWING OILING POINTS

Take out the face plate thumb screw (B, Fig. 24) and remove the face plate. Put one drop of oil into each of the oil holes and joints thus uncovered, as indicated in Fig. 25, then replace the face plate and thumb screw.

To Oil the Hook Mechanism, occasionally apply a drop of oil at the hook bearing indicated by B, in Fig. 11.

153

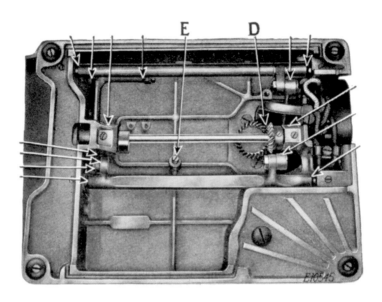

FIG. 26. OILING POINTS AT BASE OF MACHINE

To reach the parts underneath the bed of the machine, turn the machine over on its rear side. Remove the thumb nut from the screw (E, Fig. 26) at the center of the large cover plate underneath the bed of the machine and remove the cover plate. Apply oil to the oil holes and bearings indicated by the unlettered arrows in Fig. 26, and occasionally apply a small quantity of **SINGER** MOTOR LUBRICANT to the teeth of the gears (D, Fig. 26), then replace the bed cover plate and fasten it as before with the thumb nut, being careful not to turn the thumb nut too tightly.

154

To Lubricate the Motor

USE ONLY **SINGER** MOTOR LUBRICANT FOR LUBRICATING THE MOTOR. A tube of this lubricant is sent with the machine.

The **SINGER** MOTOR LUBRICANT is a specially prepared non-flowing compound which is not affected by varying temperatures. It is the only lubricant which will positively lubricate the motor. Other lubricants, including oil or ordinary grease must not be used for lubricating the motor as they are harmful for this purpose.

FIG. 27. MOTOR GREASE TUBES

When the machine is shipped from the factory, the two motor grease tubes (A, Fig. 27) are filled with sufficient **SINGER** MOTOR LUBRICANT for approximately six months use, under ordinary circumstances.

At least once every six months thereafter, these grease tubes should be refilled with the **SINGER** MOTOR LUBRICANT. To do this, insert the tip of the motor lubricant tube into the hole of each of the grease tubes and force the lubricant through each hole until both grease tubes are filled.

HINTS

Belt. See that the belt has the correct tension. The tension should be only enough to keep the belt from slipping. If the belt tension is incorrect, loosen the screw (C, Fig. 7) about one turn and allow the motor to drop downward until the belt has the correct tension, then tighten the screw (C).

Machine Working Heavily. If the machine runs hard after standing idle for some time, use a little kerosene in the oiling places, run the machine rapidly, then wipe clean and oil.

To Avoid Breaking the Needles. See that the presser foot or attachments are securely fastened by the thumb screw. Do not sew heavy seams or very thick goods with too fine a needle. A large needle and thread to correspond should be used on heavy work (see inside cover at back of book).

See that the needle is not bent, and avoid pulling the material when stitching.

Breaking of Needle Thread. If the needle thread breaks it may be caused by:

Improper threading.
Tension being too tight.
The thread being too coarse for size of needle.
The needle being bent, having a blunt point, or being set incorrectly.

Breaking of Bobbin Thread. If the bobbin thread breaks it may be caused by:

Improper threading of bobbin case.
Tension being too tight.

Skipping of Stitches. The needle may not be accurately set into the needle bar or the needle may be blunt or bent. The needle may be too small for the thread in use.

Free Instruction for using the machine is gladly given at any SINGER Shop.

INSTRUCTIONS FOR USING THE ATTACHMENTS

The Foot Hemmer

FIG. 28. THE FOOT HEMMER

The Foot Hemmer (Fig. 28) is attached to the machine in place of the presser foot. Raise the needle to its highest position, loosen the thumb screw which clamps the presser foot to the presser bar and remove the presser foot. Attach the Foot Hemmer to the bar, taking care to tighten the screw firmly so that the Hemmer will not become loose when the machine is running. Turn the balance wheel slowly to make sure that the needle goes through the center of the needle hole and that the lower thread is properly pulled up.

How to Start the Hem at the Very Edge

How to start the hem at the very edge of the material is of great importance in learning to use the Hemmer. If the hem is not started at the edge and the material is pulled bias a perfect hem cannot be made.

There are several ways of starting the hem at the edge, but the most practical one is as follows:

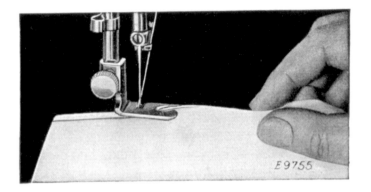

FIG. 29. STARTING A HEM AT THE EDGE

1. Fold over about ⅛″ of the edge of the material at the starting point for a distance of about one inch.

2. Place the material in the Hemmer at an angle leading to the right at a point just beyond the fold.

3. Draw the material toward you through the Hemmer, as shown in Fig. 29, at the same time making the second fold at the very edge. Continue to draw the material through the Hemmer until the edge is just under the needle. Place the upper and lower threads together under the Hemmer foot and assist in starting of the hem by slightly pulling the threads from the back as the machine is run.

Making a Hem with the Foot Hemmer

The same width of material must be kept in the Hemmer at all times. After placing the correct

FIG. 30. MAKING A HEM WITH THE FOOT HEMMER

width of material in the Hemmer hold it in a straight line and you will find it quite easy to make a perfect hem. See Fig. 30.

Making a Hemmed Seam with the Foot Hemmer

The hemmed seam is very practical to use on underwear, or in fact on any garment where a straight seam is used and where a small double seam would be suitable.

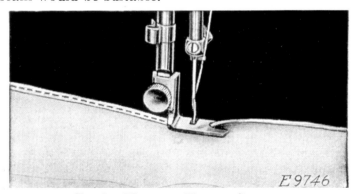

FIG. 31. MAKING A HEMMED SEAM

When using this seam, the garment must first be fitted and the edge of the material trimmed, allowing for about one-eighth inch seam. The two edges are placed together and inserted in the Hemmer in the same manner as a single hem. See Fig. 31. If the material is bulky, the edge of the upper piece of material may be placed about one-eighth inch in from the edge of the lower piece.

The free edge of a hemmed seam may be stitched flat to the garment if desired. First open the work out flat, then place the hem in the scroll of the Hemmer, which acts as a guide, holding the edge of the hem in position while it is being stitched.

If the seam is stitched flat to the garment one row of stitching is visible on the right side.

The hemmed seam may be used on muslin, lawn, percale, organdie or other fine materials where a narrow seam is desirable.

Hemming and Sewing on Lace in One Operation

Start the hem in the regular way, and with the needle holding the hem in position raise the presser

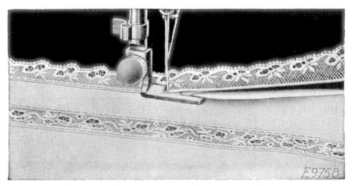

FIG. 32. HEMMING AND SEWING ON LACE

bar sufficiently to allow the edge of the lace to be slipped in under the Foot Hemmer, at the same time bringing it up through the slot at the right of the Hemmer. See Fig. 31. Lower the bar, turn the balance wheel and catch the edge of the lace with the needle. Guide the hem with the right hand and the lace with the left. Care should be taken not to stretch the lace as it is being fed into the Hemmer.

It is not practical to sew gathered lace on with the Foot Hemmer, as the fulled lace catches in the Hemmer slot.

A very attractive way of applying lace so that the stitching of the hem is not visible is to start the hem in the regular way, slipping the lace in from the left until the edge is caught in with the hem in the same manner as the upper piece of material when making a hemmed seam.

ADJUSTABLE HEMMER—Hemming

Remove the presser foot and attach the adjustable hemmer in its place, as shown in Fig. 33. This

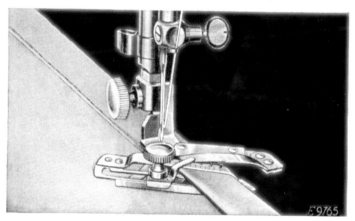

FIG. 33

hemmer will turn hems from $\frac{3}{16}$ inch to $\frac{15}{16}$ inch wide. The adjustment is made by loosening the thumb screw on the hemmer and moving the scale to the right or left until the hem turned is of the desired width. Place the cloth under the hemmer and draw the edge toward the left under the scale, as shown in Fig. 33. Draw the edge of the cloth back and forth until the fold of the hem is formed, stopping with the end under the needle. Lower the presser bar and commence to sew, being careful to so guide the cloth as to keep the hemmer full.

ADJUSTABLE HEMMER—Wide Hemming

To make a hem more than $\frac{15}{16}$ inch wide, loosen the thumb screw in the hemmer and move the scale

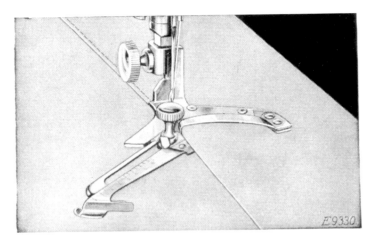

FIG. 34

to the right as far as it will go, then swing it toward you as shown in Fig. 34 and tighten the thumb screw. Fold and crease down a hem of the desired width; pass the fold under the extension at the right of the hemmer, and the edge into the folder as shown in Fig. 34, and proceed to stitch the hem.

MULTIPLE SLOTTED BINDER

This multiple slotted Binder will apply **unfolded bias binding** $\frac{15}{16}$ inch in width and commercial **folded binding** in sizes **1, 2, 3, 4** and **5** to the seams or to the edges of garments. These sizes of folded binding are $\frac{1}{4}$, $\frac{5}{16}$, $\frac{3}{8}$, $\frac{7}{16}$ and $\frac{1}{2}$ inch in width, respectively, and are fed through slots of corresponding sizes in the binder scroll. (See Fig. 35). Binding may be purchased in a variety of materials and colors.

For convenience in determining the correct width of **unfolded binding** ($\frac{15}{16}$ inch), this measurement is marked on the Binder, as shown in Fig. 35.

The two upright guide pins shown in Fig. 35 eliminate manual guiding of the binding.

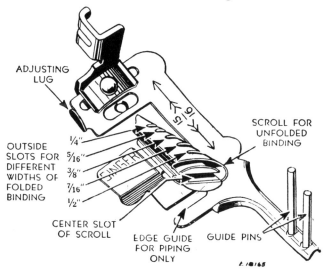

FIG. 35. MULTIPLE SLOTTED BINDER 160359

The wide range of bindings that can be applied with this Binder makes it useful for a large variety of work. It will be found particularly advantageous for making children's wear, lingerie, summer dresses, and other dainty articles which call for the narrower bindings.

As two different widths of binding of contrasting colors can be fed through the Binder at the same time, attractive bindings and piping effects can be produced in one operation.

To Attach the Binder

Raise the needle to its highest position, then attach the Binder to the presser bar in place of the presser foot.

See that the needle enters the center of the needle hole.

To Insert the Binding in the Binder

Cut all binding to a long point to the left, as shown in Fig. 36.

Folded Bias Binding must be inserted in the slot or slots of corresponding sizes. (See Fig. 39).

Unfolded or Raw Edge Bias Binding must be inserted in the open end of the scroll. (See Fig. 37).

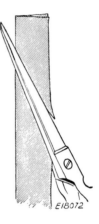

Fig. 36

After inserting the pointed end of the binding in the Binder, push it through until the full width of the binding is under the needle.

Guide the binding by means of the two upright pins, as shown in Figs. 37 and 39.

To Insert the Garment in the Binder

Place the edge to be bound as far to the right as it will go in the center slot of the scroll, as shown in Fig. 37, and draw it back under the binder foot.

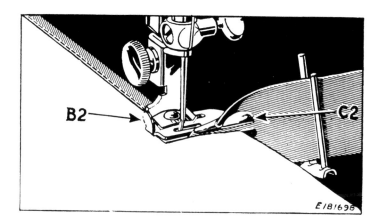

FIG. 37
BINDING WITH UNFOLDED BINDING

Lower the Binder by means of the presser foot lifter, and commence to sew. Keep the material well within the center slot of the scroll so that the edge will be caught in the binding.

To Adjust the Binder

To bring the inner edge of the binding closer to the stitching, move the scroll (C2, Fig. 37) to the right by means of the lug (B2, Fig. 37). This is the usual adjustment when binding straight edges.

When binding curves, move the scroll to the left to bring the inner edge of the binding farther from the stitching and allow for the sweep of the curve.

Piped Edge

To produce a **piped edge** on garments, move the lug (B2, Fig. 38) to the left to bring the stitching about midway of the folded binding.

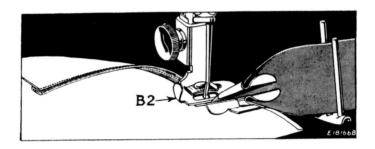

Fig. 38

Position of Garment and Binding when Piping Edges

Crease the raw edges of the garment toward the wrong side about ⅛ inch, and insert the folded edge, raw edges uppermost, into the edge guide on the Binder and **beneath** the binding.

When stitched, both sides of the garment will be finished, and the right side will show the piped edge.

Piping and Binding in One Operation

A garment can be piped and bound in one operation, as shown in Fig. 39.

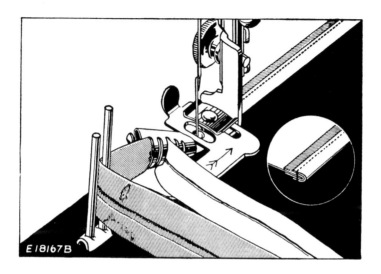

FIG. 39
PIPING AND BINDING IN ONE OPERATION

IMPORTANT: When piping and binding at the same time, as shown above, insert the **narrow width** of binding **first** in its slot, then insert the **wider width** in its slot. **Two consecutive widths should not be used at the same time.** That is, if No. 1 is used, the wider binding should not be smaller than No. 3. If No. 2 is used, the wider binding should be not less than No. 4. **Never use Nos. 1 and 2, or 2 and 3, etc., together.**

Use the upright guide pins to guide the wider of the two widths of binding, as shown in Fig. 39.

To Bind Outside Curves

Allow the edge to be bound to pass freely through the scroll without crowding against the scroll wall. The material must be guided from the back of the Binder and to the left, permitting unfinished edges to swing naturally into the scroll of the Binder.

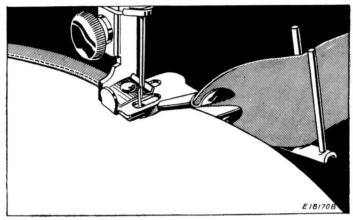

FIG. 40. BINDING AN OUTSIDE CURVE

Never pull the binding while it is being fed through the Binder, as this may stretch the binding, making it too narrow to stitch or to turn in the edges.

When binding curves, turn the material only as fast as the machine sews.

Do not push the material in too fast as this will pucker the edge.

Do not stretch the material as this will distort the edge so that the curve will not have the proper shape when finished.

If the stitching does not catch the edge of the binding, adjust the scroll slightly to the left.

To Bind Inside Curves

When binding an inside curve, straighten out the edge of the material while feeding it into the Binder, being careful not to stretch the material.

Soft materials like batiste or crepe de chine require a row of stitching added close to the edge of the curve before binding.

To Apply French Folds to Curves

Place the material under the Binder and stitch the binding onto the face of the material, as shown in Fig. 41.

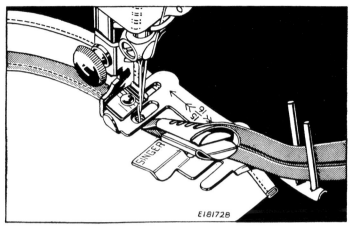

FIG. 41. APPLYING A FRENCH FOLD

For guidance in applying the rows of French folds, mark the material with a line of basting stitches or with chalk or pencil.

THE EDGE-STITCHER

This useful attachment is fastened to the machine in place of the presser foot, and will be found an indispensable aid whenever stitching must be kept accurately on the extreme edge of a piece of material. The slots, numbered from 1 to 5 in Fig. 42, serve as guides for sewing together laces, insertions and embroideries, sewing in position hemmed or folded edges, piping or sewing flat braid to a garment.

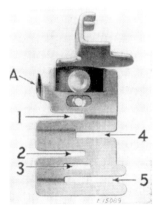

FIG. 42
THE EDGE-STITCHER

Adjusting the Edge-Stitcher

After attaching the edge-stitcher to the machine, turn the balance wheel slowly by hand to see that the needle goes through the center of the needle hole. The distance of the line of stitching from the edge of the material in the slots can be regulated by pushing the lug (A, Fig. 42) to the right or left. If it moves hard, put a drop of oil under the blue spring, then wipe it dry.

Sewing Lace Together with the Edge-Stitcher

It is difficult to sew two lace edges together even after basting, but the edge-stitcher makes it pos-

FIG. 43. SEWING LACE TOGETHER

sible to stitch on the very edge. Place one edge in slot 1 and the other in slot 4, and adjust lug (A, Fig. 42) until both edges are caught by the stitching. Hold the two pieces slightly overlapped to keep them against the ends of the slots. The thread tensions should be loose to avoid puckering of fine lace.

Lace and ribbon or other insertions can be set in by using the same slots (1 and 4, Fig. 42). The ma-

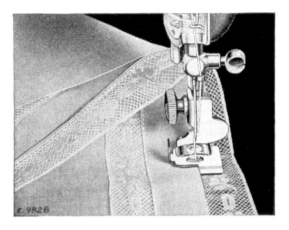

FIG. 44. SETTING IN LACE INSERTION

terial may be folded over before placing it in the slot so that a double thickness is stitched and will not pull out. The surplus material is trimmed away close to the stitching as shown in Fig. 44.

Piping with the Edge-Stitcher

Piping is very attractive if the correct contrasting color is chosen for the piping material. Place the piping with its finished edge to the left, in slot 3 (Fig. 42). Place the edge to be piped in slot 4, as shown in Fig. 45.

Piping should preferably be cut bias, and should be cut to twice the width of the slot (3, Fig. 42) in the edge-stitcher so that it can be folded once.

Applying Bias Folds with the Edge-Stitcher

Folded bias tape or military braid, used for neat and colorful trimming, may be sewn on by placing the garment under the edge-stitcher the same as under a presser foot, and placing the tape in slot 1 or 4 (Fig. 42). To make a square corner, sew until the turning point is reached, then remove the tape from the attachment and form the corner by hand, replace it in the slot and continue stitching, as

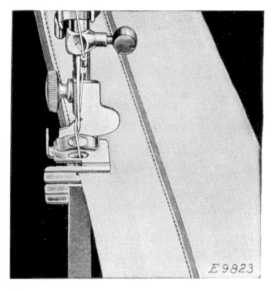

FIG. 45. PIPING WITH THE EDGE-STITCHER

shown in Fig. 46. To space two or more parallel rows, a guide line such as a crease, chalk mark or basting thread should be used.

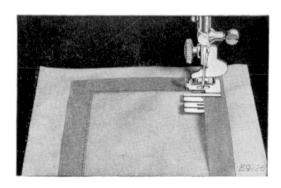

FIG. 46. APPLYING BIAS FOLDS WITH THE EDGE-STITCHER

Stitching a Wide Hem with the Edge-Stitcher

A wide hem on sheets, pillow slips, etc., may be stitched evenly with the edge-stitcher after the hem

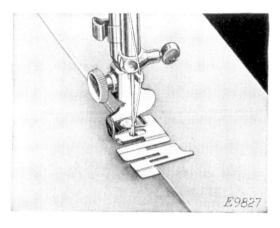

FIG. 47. MAKING A WIDE HEM

has been measured and the edge turned. Insert the edge in slot 5 as shown in Fig. 47 and adjust to stitch as close to the edge as desired.

Making a French Seam

An even French seam may be made by inserting the two edges to be joined, wrong sides together, in slot 1 or 2 and stitching close to the edge; then folding both right sides together and inserting the back of the seam into slot 1 again and stitching with just enough margin to conceal the raw edges. See Fig. 48.

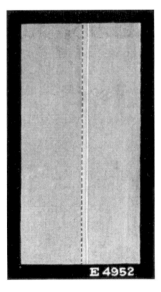

FIG. 48. A FRENCH SEAM

173

Tucking with the Edge-Stitcher

Dainty narrow tucking may be produced on the edge-stitcher by inserting creased folds in slot 1 as

FIG. 49. TUCKING WITH THE EDGE-STITCHER

shown in Fig. 49, and adjusting the edge-stitcher to right or left for the desired width of tuck, up to $\frac{1}{8}$ inch. Successive tucks may be easily creased by folding the material at the desired distance from the previous tuck, and then running the length of the fold over a straight edge such as the edge of the sewing machine cabinet. The secret of good tucking lies in a light tension, short stitch, and fine thread and needle.

174

SHIRRING WITH THE GATHERER

The gatherer is fastened to the machine in the same manner as the presser foot. Material placed under the gatherer and stitched in the usual way will be slightly gathered. Any fabric that drapes well is especially suited for shirring with the gatherer. Most shirring with the gatherer is done with a long stitch and tight tension. To increase the fullness of the gathers, lengthen the stitch. To decrease the fullness, shorten the stitch.

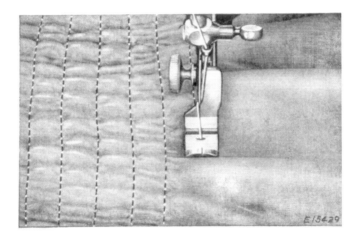

FIG. 50. THE GATHERER IN OPERATION

With the gatherer, it is possible to shirr in narrow rows as shown in Fig. 50. The material may be guided as easily as when sewing with the presser foot. Fine materials, such as batiste, silk or net, may be very attractively shirred. Where only a slight fullness is required, as at the top of a sleeve or around the neck, the gatherer will be found very convenient.

175

FIG. 51. SHIRRING

A very pleasing effect may be gained by using thread or embroidery silk of contrasting color on the bobbin. Fig. 52 shows a white organdie collar and cuff set with red and green smocking made with the gatherer, using fine crochet cotton or tatting thread on the top and white cotton on the bobbin.

FIG. 52. SMOCKING

176

RUFFLER

Lines 1, 2, 3, 4 and 5 shown in Fig. 53 indicate where the material is to be placed for various operations, as follows:

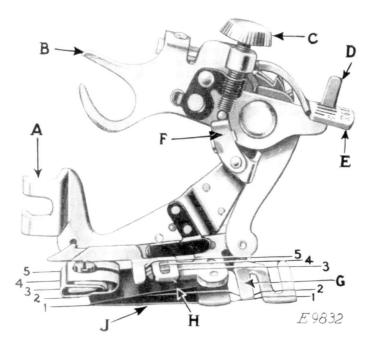

FIG. 53. THE RUFFLER AND ITS PARTS

Line 1—the correct position for the material to which the ruffled material is applied.
Line 2—material to be ruffled.
Line 3—the facing for the ruffle.
Line 4—the strip of piping material.
Line 5—the edge to be piped.

Refer to Fig. 53 when inserting the material in the ruffler.

177

The names and uses of the principal parts of the ruffler are as follows:

(SEE REFERENCES IN FIG. 53)

A—FOOT—the part by which the ruffler is attached to the presser bar.

B—FORK ARM—the section that must be placed astride the needle clamp.

C—ADJUSTING SCREW—the screw that regulates the fullness of the gather.

D—PROJECTION—the part that projects through the slots in the adjusting lever.

E—ADJUSTING LEVER—the lever that sets the ruffler for gathering or for making a plait once at every six stitches or once at every twelve stitches, as desired; also for disengaging the ruffler, when either plaiting or gathering is not desired.

F—ADJUSTING FINGER—the part which regulates the width or size of the plaits.

G—SEPARATOR GUIDE—the guide on the underside of the ruffler, containing slots into which the edge of the material is placed to keep the heading of the ruffle even; also for separating the material to be ruffled from the material to which the ruffle is to be attached.

H—RUFFLING BLADE—the upper blue steel blade with the teeth at the end to push the material in plaits up to the needle.

J—SEPARATOR BLADE—the lower blue steel blade without teeth, which prevents the teeth of the ruffling blade coming into contact with the feed of the machine or the material to which ruffle or plaiting is to be applied.

To Attach the Ruffler to the Machine

Raise the needle bar to its highest position and remove the presser foot. Attach the ruffler foot (A, Fig. 53) to the presser bar from the right and fasten by means of the thumb screw, at the same time placing the fork arm (B, Fig. 53) astride the needle clamp as shown in Fig. 54.

To Adjust the Ruffler for Gathering

The adjusting finger (F, Fig. 54) is not intended for gathering and should be moved forward or away from the needle, as shown in Fig. 54.

FIG. 54

Raise the adjusting lever (E, Fig. 54) and move it to the left so that the projection (D, Fig. 54) will enter the slot marked "1" in the adjusting lever (E) when the lever is released. The ruffling blade will then move forward and back once at every stitch. Insert the material to be ruffled between the two blue blades, following the line 2 in Fig. 53. Draw the material slightly back of the needle, lower the presser bar and commence to sew.

To make fine gathering, shorten the stroke of the ruffling blade by turning the adjusting screw (C, Fig. 54) upward; also shorten the stitch. To make full gathering, lengthen the stroke of the ruffling blade by turning the adjusting screw (C) downward; also lengthen the stitch. By varying these adjustments, many pleasing varieties of work can be accomplished.

To Make a Ruffle and Sew it to a
Garment in One Operation

Insert the material to be ruffled between the two
blue blades, as shown in Fig. 55, following the line

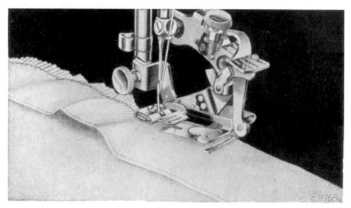

FIG. 55

2, in Fig. 53. Place the garment to which the
ruffle is to be attached, under the separator blade,
following the line 1, in Fig. 53. Proceed the same
as for gathering.

The edge of the ruffled seam can later be bound
by using the Binder.

To Ruffle and Sew on a Facing
in One Operation

Insert the material to be ruffled between the two
blue blades, following the line 2, in Fig. 53. Place
the garment to which the ruffle is to be attached
under the separator blade, following the line 1, in
Fig. 53. Place the material for the facing over the
upper blue blade, as shown in Fig. 56, following
the line 3, in Fig. 53. The facing may be straight
or bias material. If the facing is to be on the
right side of the garment, place the garment and

the ruffle so that the wrong sides are together. If the facing is to be on the wrong side, place the right sides of the garment and the ruffle together.

FIG. 56

Piping a Ruffle

Insert the material to be ruffled between the two blue blades, following the line 2, in Fig. 53. This

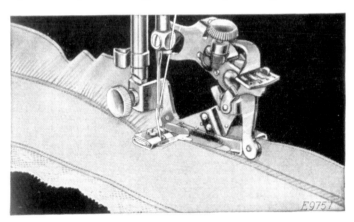

FIG. 57

material must not be over 1¼ inches wide, as it is carried through the ruffler with the finished edge of the ruffle to the right of the attachment as shown in Fig. 57.

The material for piping must measure about ¼ inch wide when folded in the center and is usually cut on the bias. Place the piping material in the ruffler, following the line 4, in Fig. 53, with the folded edge of the piping to the right. The material to which the piping and ruffling are to be sewn should be folded on the edge and inserted in the ruffler, following the line 5, in Fig. 53.

To Adjust the Ruffler for Plaiting

Raise the adjusting lever (E, Fig. 58) and move it to the right so that the projection (D, Fig. 58)

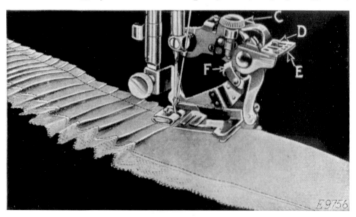

Fig. 58

will enter the slot marked "6" in the adjusting lever when the lever is released. The ruffling blade will then move forward and back once at every six stitches. To adjust the ruffling blade to make a plait once at every twelve stitches, place the adjusting lever (E, Fig. 58) so that the projection (D) enters the slot marked "12" in the adjusting lever. Insert the material to be plaited between the two blue blades, following the line 2 (Fig. 53). The size or width of plaits is regulated by the adjusting screw

(C, Fig. 58) and the adjusting finger (F, Fig. 58). To make a wider plait, move the adjusting finger (F) back or toward the needle and turn the adjusting screw (C) downward. To make a smaller plait, turn the adjusting screw (C) upward. The distance between the plaits is regulated by the length of stitch.

To Adjust the Ruffler for
Group Plaiting and Gathering

The ruffler can be adjusted for group plaiting by lifting the adjusting lever (E, Fig. 59) and moving

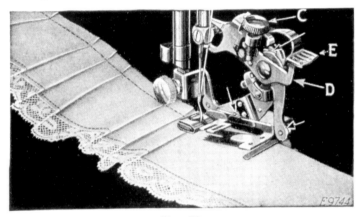

FIG. 59

it to the right so that the top of the projection (D, Fig. 59) enters the small slot indicated by the star on the adjusting lever. This should be done at the points where you wish to make the space between the plaits. The ruffler will then stop and plain stitching will be made. When the desired space has been made, adjust the lever (E) so that the projection (D) enters either the slot marked "6" or the slot marked "12." By alternately making groups of plaits and plain spaces, as shown in Fig. 59, very attractive work can be produced.

FEATHERWEIGHT 221
THE PERFECT PORTABLE®
Preface to the Expanded Third Edition

"It absolutely defines the word *classic*."

I started my love affair with *Featherweights* over ten years ago; I was hooked then and I'm still hooked today! And while I use other sewing machines as a quilt teacher and lecturer I find myself coming back again and again to use the Perfect Portable. Pick up a *Featherweight*, and you can't help but marvel that its design is older than television, the gas-powered lawn mower, fluorescent lights and the vast majority of its owners. It absolutely defines the word *classic*. The machines smell sweetly of oil and time, and they carry honest scratches and wear from long forgotten piecework. If anything, *Featherweights* have gotten better, incrementally, with age.

And the legend lives on and on. One of the most interesting aspects of the *Featherweight* saga is that virtually no one back in the dim era of the 'thirties foresaw its allure and the demand for these superb sewing machines almost seventy years later! A measure of its incredible success is the fact that, at a time when computer controlled wonders can create the most intricate stitching, the simple but efficient *Featherweight* remains as one of the most recognized and sought after sewing machines in the world.

Few things stand still in time, and historical or technical works like this book are no exception. Over the few years since I wrote the first edition of the Featherweight 221 book in 1992, the wealth of knowledge on these wonderful sewing machines had literally exploded. Talk about *Featherweights* became common at Quilt Guilds, in sewing rooms, flea markets and even on Internet chat rooms. Increased recognition and awakened enthusiasm fostered serious study of the *Featherweight* by owners and collectors everywhere. In any field or art, appreciation increases with knowledge about the subject. More and more people began to value the *Featherweight 221* sewing machine as a highly practical portable, as a family heirloom, a significant bit of Americana, or just for its simple but impressive mechanical attributes.

To reflect all this new information I revised and updated the original version of the Featherweight book with a second edition in 1997. In that sequel I compiled much personal research along with valuable contributions made to me by people all over the world. The result was a labor of love: an expanded edition of 184 pages, with nineteen chapters packed with the most up-to-date information on the Perfect Portable as it's typically seen, as well as in its rare limited edition variations. Some myths were dispelled in its pages, and additional technical information was included. In the second book my goal was to combine personal glimpses and vignettes with the more practical features of a technical work. I was, and am, happy with the outcome, and interest and demand in what's been called "The Featherweight Book" continues to this day.

But time marches on. Some new information on *Featherweights* has come to light over the past five years. I've received more than 250 additional letters, some with testimonials and many others with bits and pieces of new data. And Model 221 enthusiasts continue to call and write for help in sorting out "what they have". So, to continue to document the *Featherweight* legend I've decided to go for a third edition - by including a Supplement with newly surfaced information. The Supplement follows in the pages after this short Preface. I've been working on it at odd moments as I've had time over the past three years, and once again I asked my husband, Frank, to help get my manuscript into print. I couldn't have done it otherwise - since I just completed a new quilting book, *Block Magic*, and as I write these lines I'm working on another quilt book that's scheduled for 2003.

I express my heartfelt thanks to all who have made this expanded edition possible. Almost ten years ago when I wrote the original Featherweight Book, it stood alone as the only book on the legendary Model 221 sewing machine. The second, and now this third edition, continues that status. And I promise to revise, update and expand this book as important new information becomes available. A decade-long love affair is just too hard to shrug off!

THIRD EDITION SUPPLEMENT

I In writing this Supplement I have decided to index it using subtitles for the newest information. I've also included page numbers to reference back to the original text that appears earlier in this book. Readers should note that each section is written with a "stand alone" flavor for those who might skip pages because they are only interested in a specific section.

The Featherweight Name (also see page 17)

I continued to be intrigued by the name Featherweight and did some additional research on it. Before World War Two the name wasn't used in *Singer* advertising or machine brochures. Our favorite machine was referred to as the Model 221 Portable or Portable Electric. I started seeing the Featherweight name in circa-1945 advertisements as the war was winding down and *Singer* was showing what women could expect in "Your Post-war Singer". But it was hit and miss; sometimes in the ad, other times not. Shirley McElderry from Iowa collects old periodicals and concentrates on needlework-related ones. She confirmed that in the Summer 1946 issue of the McCall Needlework magazine, a Model 221 machine is shown in the ad but it's not referred to as a Featherweight. The Winter 1947/48 advertisement in the same magazine showed a "*Singer featherweight portable*" (featherweight not capitalized). It was not until the Summer 1949 issue that an advertisement in McCall's referred to the "*Singer Featherweight Portable - outsells any other model in the world; weighs 11 pounds*". Compare this history with an ad in the December, 1946 edition of the Canadian Home Journal. *Singer* advertised, "*This Christmas there will be Singers under the tree.... Now in Canada - an 11 pound 2oz. wonder that behaves like an angel!.... The Singer Featherweight Portable Electric*".

When I researched it in 1996 *Singer* had a trademark on the Mark Featherweight with respect to sewing machines. But in the late '40s and early '50s other portables (made by competitors) were advertised using the Featherweight name. How can this be? I'm not sure. Possibly there was a dispute that "featherweight" is in the public domain, and it was eventually resolved in *Singer's* favor. Or maybe *Singer* filed for registration of the Mark at a later time. There is one curiosity, though, with respect to Trademark Law. Owners of registered Marks are required to use the symbol ® at the first occurrence of the word(s) in advertising, pamphlets, etc. But typically *Singer* did not follow this convention. Often the word Featherweight is used without any reference to a trademark. But when it is referenced it is always with an asterisk (*) following the word Featherweight. Then, when you refer to the asterisk you'll find a statement to the effect that *Featherweight* is a Trademark of *The Singer Manufacturing Company.* Interesting!

Historical Perspectives (also see pages 23 - 25)

I have always wondered about the role of the *Featherweight* in World War Two, also about the war's impact on a company like the *Singer Sewing Machine Company.* I've already written at length about the black crinkle machines and the "blackside" *Featherweights* that are tied to that period of time. But what of the company itself and the more common "Plain Jane" machines?

Beginning with the birth of the *Featherweight* and into the early 1940's, the *Singer* Company had developed significant physical and human resources at its Elizabethport Works. The plant was entirely self sufficient, with it's own power house, foundry, tooling department, testing laboratories, plating and painting sections, photography and printing, and even shuttle trucks and trailers for its warehousing operation. All these functions served the core manufacturing operation, with aisle upon aisle of machine tools, bins and assembly benches. Most of the smaller components such as screws, springs, nuts and pins were produced within the facility. The plant also had a large pool of skilled employees who were routinely involved in designing, producing and assembling a high volume of precision-fitted machine parts. Its foremen and supervisory staff were remembered as being particularly effective. All told, the *Singer* Elizabethport Works was a model, high-volume manufacturing facility in the period preceding World War Two.

The war began in Europe in 1939 and Great Britain became involved almost immediately. *Singer's* factory at Clydebank, Scotland, was enlisted for the production of war goods. Shops and stores around the world that were previously supplied by Clydebank transferred their orders to the network originating at the factory in Elizabethport, New Jersey. In addition, sales outlets in the U.S. began to foresee the possibility of this country's involvement. Increased demand for *Featherweights* and other sewing machines turned up the pressure on Elizabethport. But with war looming, materials such as chromium, nickel, aluminum and copper began to dry up for civilian needs, and production of sewing machines became increasingly difficult. James Slaten from California sent me a good reference paper. It related that three months after the U.S. entered the war, the War Production Board advised *Singer* that the manufacture of all household sewing machines was to be discontinued in June of 1942. Limitation Order L-98 prohibited the manufacture of all such sewing machines from then until July 1945. In addition, the inventory of household sewing machines at Elizabethport was frozen and no further shipments were authorized except to agencies of the government or to certain foreign accounts, mainly in South America, in support of our national policy interests. Conversely, the output of industrial sewing machines was increased to supply the needs of the military garment industry. The Elizabethport Works also began to manufacture wartime goods, including the U.S. military model pistol. Even the *Singer Manufacturing Company's* cabinet factory at South Bend, Indiana was pressed into vital war work.

For the duration of the war, there was a shortage of garments in the stores, so women who had never sewn before began to repair and even make clothing. *Singer* offered more sewing classes and emphasized its machine rental service because the average woman only needed a sewing machine for a few hours now and then. The *Featherweight* became the workhorse of this rental pool because it was so small and handy, and it would perform well under the demands of back-to-back rentals by new sewers. *Singer* advertised in newspapers and women's journals for "idle machines" in order to recondition and sell them to families with ongoing needs for a sewing machine. The company even made priority treatment certificates available to sellers, if they wanted to buy a machine when civilian manufacture resumed in the post-war period. *Featherweights* in particular were in high demand because wives moved with their husbands (and few home furnishings) to domestic posts. Also, *Featherweights* traveled with adventurous women who were in search of "Rosie the Riveter" type work. Many of the pre-war *Featherweights* in the AD through AF series show the marks and scratches from long, hard service during this critical period in our nation's history. They probably merit a crisp salute!

221K7 Timing Belt drive (also see pages 29 - 30)

Frank was at a Quilt Show with me last year and he saw a white-colored *Featherweight* on a vendor's table. A potential buyer was looking at it and a small group was watching so he joined in to listen to the sales talk. After a while the buyer's husband spoke up and started talking about its belt drive. Frank was surprised to hear the man say something to the effect that repairmen do not like the white *Featherweight* because they can't dip the machine in cleaning solvent without damaging the rubber belt. This raised some eyebrows. Whether his statement was made to try to get the price reduced, or because he heard it somewhere and was just repeating it, we'll never know.

Neither of us heard anything like this before. Over the years some repairmen had wondered about the longevity of the timing belt design as compared with solid gears, but found out it held up well. But this cleaning solvent bath was a new perspective. We talked again with a few of our trade contacts that had extensive experience with *Featherweights*. One laughed after hearing the story and asked what would happen to the plastic parts like the light switch, bobbin winder wheel and the stitch length adjuster knob. Wouldn't they dissolve in the solvent? Another serviceman questioned if the motor and foot controller wires would withstand the bath. All agreed that trying to clean something like a *Featherweight* machine by dipping in a solvent bath was definitely not the norm for the trade.

I mention this story here to help assure readers that the white-colored 221K7 *Featherweight* is a high quality sewing machine with an excellent reputation. Yes, it's a little different because it was designed to compete in an increasingly cost-conscious world. But the design has given long and trouble-free service to countless women since it was introduced. And it's still doing it!

Beige (Tan) Machines (also see pages 30 - 32)
Last year a Pennsylvania woman wrote to me about her first machine. She enclosed some photos of a beige *Featherweight*, with the regular beige/brown trim carrying case and an instruction book marked for the 221K5 machine. All this is typical. But then I looked closely; the model identification plate under the medallion said 221K instead of 221J. And when I read her letter I found that the machine has serial number EV 967437.

Yes, I know that the 221J machine is just a model designation for the 221K5 painted in beige, but this is the first one I've seen that had anything but an ES, ET or JE prefix for its serial number. Also, it's one of only three beige machines I'm aware of that have the 221K model identification plate, rather than one that reads 221J or 221J6. The other two have the ES prefix.

Referring to its serial number, this EV machine was made at Clydebank, Scotland in early 1964. That is about 1-1/2 years later than the last beige machine from the factory's ET prefix run. How many beige 221K5's were made is unknown. Possibly it was a "parts cleanup" operation; the factory had already been producing the new 221K7 (white) *Featherweight* for some time. Also, just how the EV 221K machine compares in sequence with the JE prefix machines from St. Johns, Canada is open to speculation. One source reports that the JE prefix was used at St. Johns starting in about 1964. If this is true, the Pennsylvania beige 221K is probably a precursor to the JE prefix machines that were assembled or manufactured in Canada. So this would expand the years during which beige *Featherweights* were made. Previously I had thought it was from about 1960 into 1962; so this estimate would change to something like 1960 to 1965. On the other hand, if the JE prefix was used at St. John's earlier than 1964, then the Pennsylvania 221K machine would be from a much later, second run at Clydebank. Hopefully, additional data to confirm the timing of the St. Johns' prefixes will come to light in the future. I've received many letters and calls on these desirable beige machines and it would be nice to give a definitive answer on the birthdates of the Canadian JE series *Featherweights*.

Model 211K and 222K Birthdates (also see page 39)

In the second edition I included two tables to allow owners to determine the approximate date of manufacture of their Model 221 U.S. machine. There was another table for the Model 221K and 222K *Featherweights* made at the Kilbowie factory in Clydebank, Scotland. The tables remain largely accurate; however since then I've been able to get more information on the manufacturing dates of *Featherweights* made in Great Britain. It's from a copy of the Singer Sewing Machine Recognition Manual by the *Singer Company (U.K.) Ltd.*, 1982. I also used research notes compiled by the Library & Museums Department at the Central Library in Clydebank, Scotland.

Beginning in 1900, the convention at the *Singer* Clydebank factory was to change the prefix letter (what I call the machine's series letter) every two years. Serial numbering was restarted each time the series letter was changed, with 000001 being the first number. However, in the *Featherweight* production years, the time between series letter changes varied considerably, as will be seen in the following table.

Series Letter	Start - End
EA	October 1935 - January 1937
EB	February 1937 - January 1939
EC	February 1939 - December 1940
ED	January 1941 - April 1947
EE	April 1947 - February 1949
EF	March 1949 - September 1950
EG	September 1950 - December 1951
EH	December 1951 - June 1953
EJ	June 1953 - November 1954
EK	November 1954 - January 1956
EL	January 1956 - December 1956
EM	December 1956 - December 1957
EN	January 1958 - February 1959
EP	February 1959 - March 1960
ER	March 1960 - October 1960
ES	October 1960 - October 1961
ET	October 1961 - December 1962
EV	December 1962 - July 1964
EW	*allocated to the Bridgeport Programme 1962-1970*
EX	July 1964 - October 1966
EY	October 1966 - October 1968
EZ	May 1968 - April 1970
FA	*no mention of the FA series at Clydebank*
FB	April 1969 - June 1971
FC	June 1971 - August 1972
FD	September 1972 - February 1974

Astute readers will note that Singer-U.K. skipped the EI, EO and EQ series at Clydebank, just as the U.S. Elizabethport factory did not use the AI series prefix. Why? It seems logical that this was to avoid confusion between the letter I, and the letter L or the number one; likewise with the letters O and Q between themselves or with the number zero. I will write more on this in the next section.

The FA series belt-driven *Featherweights* remain as a bit of a mystery - as the machines, foot controllers and even the instruction books are clearly marked "Made in Great Britain". However, the Clydebank serial number records from the *Singer (U.K.)* Manual do not show that series. Possibly this is an error on the part of the historians. On the other hand, there is speculation that the *Singer* factory at Clydebank did not <u>manufacture</u> the machines with FA serial numbers. It is opinioned that they were just <u>assembled</u> in Great Britain from parts that were produced in the Far East or elsewhere. This might have raised an eyebrow in the late sixties or early seventies. However, in today's global economy this sourcing would not surprise me in the least. The FA series machines were marketed in Great Britain beginning in about 1968. The U.K. instruction booklets are printed with a 1967 date.

A woman told me she heard different dates than the ones I list here. She said it was October 1968 to April of 1969 for the EZ series, and May 1969 to April 1970 for the FA series. My correspondent wasn't sure what the information was based on, so I'm mentioning it in this section purely for academic purposes. However, a correspondent in South Carolina owns a 221K7 machine with serial number FA 126588 that she received as a birthday present while in college in October 1969. It doesn't seem likely that so many machines could have been manufactured between May of 1969 and her birthday! So the May 1969 start date that was quoted is probably suspect.

Once again, the reader should keep in mind that weeks, months or even years may have elapsed between the date of manufacture of a particular machine, and the date it was sold in a retail store. Therefore, the so-called birthdate of a machine may not be representative of when a *Featherweight* you own was first purchased at a *Singer* store.

Series AI Featherweight (also see pages 38 - 39)
In the earlier editions of this book I stated that I had never seen a series AI *Featherweight*. Nor had I heard of one in all my research. So

I did not include an AI series in the manufacturing date charts for U.S. machines. Then, just after the second edition was introduced I received a letter from a man in Texas who buys and sells *Featherweights*. He thought I would like to know that the AI series machines did exist - because his wife owned one! His letter included the serial number of her machine, complete with all six digits, and he reported that it had the striated face plate and a throat plate with seam allowance markings in 1/8" increments.

I was pretty excited with this information and wrote back explaining that his letter arrived too late for consideration in the second edition. I also asked for a close-up photo or a pencil tracing to include in the next Featherweight book update. A month went by. Then his reply came. It said he had tried to do a pencil tracing but must have moved some old oil or gunk while doing it. Lo and behold, the letter I became an L, so the machine was actually a series AL *Featherweight*.

A couple of years later a woman from California wrote to me. Her daughter had given her a copy of the Featherweight book. In reading through it she found the machine dating charts and discovered that her machine, which she purchased new in 1950, did belong to the Series AI. She thought I would like to know. Hope springs eternal! Once again I was excited but admittedly a bit skeptical. I wrote to her asking for a pencil tracing. Her reply was disappointing; she said that the "lower part of the L doesn't show well". Apparently it wasn't stamped too deeply.

All told, it doesn't appear that *Singer* ever used the letter I to indicate a machine Series, either for the U.S. production or at Clydebank. As I speculated earlier, it's just too easy to confuse the letter I with the letter L.

Face Plate Change-outs (pages 41 - 43)

Students of *Featherweights* know that the black 221 machines were fitted with two very different face plates - one of the earlier scrollwork designs, or the more modern striated type. Often an older machine that was originally fitted with the scrollwork plate is found with a striated one. And occasionally the opposite is seen, i.e., a newer machine with a scrollwork face plate.

The most common reason for the first scenario is that the lower thread guide on the face plate was broken off while in use. This guide is held on with a tiny rivet and most repairmen would be able to reattach it. But if the rivet were lost, the easiest fix would be to replace the faceplate. After the late 1940's the scrollwork face plate was obsolete so the replacement was undoubtedly a striated one.

When a later machine is found with a scrollwork face plate it is usually because its owner liked the earlier design better and was able to swap it out at the *Singer* store when buying the machine. Several former salesmen told me they were more than accommodating to "make the sale" by switching face plates from a new or used machine to another one.

The Perfect Indestructible Portable (also see pages 52 - 55)

The "Finding a Featherweight" chapter in my second edition stimulated more letters, many from folks who found their machine in very unusual ways. Two women found theirs on highways where the machine apparently bounced or fell from a moving pickup truck. Both ran perfectly without any repairs whatsoever. One man discovered his at a landfill as he was dumping some roofing material from a home repair. He said the Caterpillar that was working there had already run over the machine once, but fortunately it was lying on some trash bags that cushioned the weight of the 'dozer. It had a couple of deep gashes but the local repairman touched them up with black enamel when he tuned it up. His wife uses it a few times every week. Other stories were equally entertaining.

With these reports for background, I want to include one of the most interesting tales in this edition - to underscore the amazing durability of the wonderful *Featherweight*. Sandra Barrett of British Columbia has my all-time favorite story. Her husband is a heavy equipment operator who runs excavators and does lot clearing and digging for home construction. One day she came home to find a dirt and rust encrusted *Featherweight* on her front doorstep. She wrote that her husband found the machine while working that day, and that "there was not one moving part on this machine, words alone cannot describe the condition it was in, you just have to imagine the worst!" Luckily her husband knew what it was and didn't overlook it. But, "the machine to my mind was a goner - who knows how long it had been buried out there in all kinds of weather, for how many years and why?" The next morning there was a sweet aroma in the house as her husband drenched the machine in penetrating oil on a heap of newspapers. This process went on for days. She managed to pry the bobbin case out - "a complete ball of rust"- and clean it up with fine emery paper. Her hubby disassembled and cleaned some of the parts using an owner's manual as a guide. After about two weeks of soaking and cleaning they reassembled it and plugged in the foot controller from another *Featherweight*. The most unbelievable thing happened; "it worked!" After that they started the fine-tuning and were able to get good tension and an even stitch. Is this the end of the story? No, not yet! Several months later her husband was on the same property to burn the debris left over from the original land-clearing job. He saw something familiar sticking out of one of the piles. Out came the original electric cords and foot controller. Guess what? 'They worked too". Sandra wrote that she thinks I should add one more adjective - "The Perfect Indestructible Portable".

Finding a Free Arm Machine (also see pages 59 - 64)

If you're looking for a *Model 222K Featherweight Convertible,* you may want to enlist help from a friend or relative in Canada. And if you're vacationing there, spend some time looking at the newspaper ads, searching the shops and visiting tag sales. Many of the Free Arm machines that are currently making the rounds between auction houses and collectors here in the U.S. were found in Canada. Why? It's because they originated at the Clydebank site in Great Britain and were heavily marketed through its distribution network, mainly in the U.K. and former British countries. A correspondent from British Columbia wrote that 222K's are "in good supply in this region" and that she already sent one good machine to the states and has access to several more. Another comment from the north is that 'we have access to many 222's and 221's, all are open to offers". I've heard similar reports from folks in Australia and New Zealand, but by far the most encouraging and frequent ones are from residents of Canada.

Unfortunately, the days of finding a twenty-five dollar "steal" on a 222K (or 221) are mostly gone. Oh, I still hear of one occasionally but they are few and far between. More and more people are familiar with *Featherweights* and what the market will bear. As I write this, a 222K machine will command between $700. and $1800., depending on condition. An absolutely mint condition Free Arm will possibly sell for more.

Just how do you get a Free Arm machine from someone in Canada? If you find one while vacationing, just declare it at the border and pay the import duty (if any). Depending on its cost and the value of any other purchases, the total may not exceed your personal exemption. Another way is to look for one at a stateside Quilt Show or seminar that's within driving distance of Canada. You can generally find a machine or two that's been brought to the event by a Canadian vendor. In this case, the seller pays the import duty. Finally, you can buy one from home and have it shipped. Here you would make contact through advertising on the Internet, in magazines, by word of mouth, or whatever. After you commit to the machine and send the money, the seller fills out customs forms for the package at their end. Sooner or later the machine arrives at your door via the parcel delivery service or the mail.

All told, it's worth the effort to find one. *Singer* once advertised the 222K as its "Treble-Two". Some folks here in the states have dubbed it the "triple deuce". The machine is a marvel; it can do all the legendary *Featherweight* can do, and more. Anne Morgan bought hers in 1955 and traveled extensively with her husband and family in friendly and hostile places throughout the world. She made and repaired clothes, darned, embroidered, monogrammed and once made some sandals for desert wear out of tent canvas. Now she's machine quilting with hers. The final sentences of her letter sum up the 222K Free Arm machine for me. "I've done everything possible and more with my little portable. It was by far the best purchase I've ever made".

Years of Manufacture

222K machines were never manufactured along with regular 221's at Elizabethport, nor at *Singer's* Anderson or Bridgeport factories. They all originated at the Kilbowie factory in Scotland. In the previous edition I listed 1954 to 1960 as the dates of production of the machine. Since then I've received reports of later machines so I'll expand the range into 1961. Most of the years are fairly well represented but 1958 into early 1959 (EN series) seems to be a sparse production year. Why this is I do not know. Possibly a large surplus of *Featherweight Convertibles* was built up the year before; or maybe sales had dropped off during that series run.

Stateside sales of the 222K

One topic that's open to speculation is the sale of the Free Arm machine in the U.S. The *Convertible* was only made at Clydebank so it had to be imported for sale in the states. But sales were dismal, only 1267 machines from the start of marketing in 1954 through the first quarter of 1959. There is an ongoing belief that *Singer* was only pushing its U.S. manufactured machines at the time, resulting in weak U.S. sales of 222K's. Another theory is there was a balance of trade treaty to restrict imports from Great Britain, thus the only 222K machines that were sold here were "special ordered" to meet individual requests by customers. I do not believe either one. I have access to sales figures showing that in the same time period the Clydebank site was sourcing many 99 and 206 class sewing machines, along with lesser numbers of its 15, 201, and 306 class machines, into the *Singer U.S.* sales network. I also have a copy of a stateside sales brochure on "*The New Singer Featherweight Convertible*" that is dated 1953 and is "printed in the USA".

I am convinced that the weak U.S. sales of the 222K resulted from one main factor. The machine did not offer what American housewives were looking for at the time. *Singer* would have imported more Free Arm machines from Clydebank if they were selling them. The network was already in place and the company was doing it to supply other models. But U.S. women didn't want to buy Free Arm machines that couldn't do zigzag stitching. New wave machines had appeared that had a free arm and zigzag capability. And those limited few who were looking for plain, straight stitch portable machines were hard pressed to pay a premium for the 222K over the regular Model 221. Zigzags hurt the sales of regular *Featherweights* as well. In the states, *Singer* had sold over 100,000 Model 221's each year from 1950 through 1954. However, in 1955 it was about 76,000, in 1956 about 53,000, and only about 40,000 in 1957.

Embroidery Hoop

A genuine *Singer* accessory for the 222K Free Arm machine is its Embroidery Hoop. The hoop looks like a small magnifying glass, with an open area where the lens would be on the magnifier. In use, the hoop is attached to the special *Convertible* throat plate using a small screw. The Darning and Embroidery Hoop is part number 171074. It was not supplied with the machine but was available separately as an accessory.

How many Free Arms?

I still haven't been able to get a production total just for the 222K Free Arm machines. The problem is that serial numbers for

Featherweight Convertibles were inter-mixed at Clydebank with regular 221K machine runs. However, I do have most of the actual U.S. sales numbers for 222K's from *Singer's* archives. So, for the second edition I did a <u>rough estimate</u> of 222K Free Arm machine production, using the U.S. sales figures, and extrapolating by using the proportion of domestic letters referencing 222K's I had received, as compared with letters from outside the U.S. A statistician helped me with this, and it was (and is) valid practice. At that time I had four times as many letters from abroad as from the states, so I estimated the total production of 222K's at about 10,000 machines. Anyone interested in the calculation should reference back to pages 63 and 64 of this book.

Since then a *Featherweight* enthusiast told me he'd heard that another source was estimating the 222K Free Arm production at about 100,000 machines, or ten times the number I had calculated. No explanation or supporting data was offered to help confirm this number. I have no idea how this estimate was derived so I'm mentioning it here just to be complete. However, at this point I cannot subscribe to it.

My second edition stimulated more letters and calls about 222K's from all over the world. Most of them were from the U.K., Canada, Australia and New Zealand. In sum, the proportion is now about 12 to 1. So I went back to the calculator. Using the same calculations as referenced earlier I came up with just short of 25,000 machines for the total production of the desirable Treble-Two machine. Is this the final word? Probably not. As I mentioned it's only an estimate based on the database that's available. One thing is for sure though. The *Featherweight Convertible Model 222K* is one of the most useful and desirable variations of this wonderful sewing machine you can own!

1934 Century of Progress (also see pages 65 - 66)

In my second edition I wrote about the 1934 Century of Progress *Featherweight* that commemorated the Chicago World's Fair. I included historical perspective for background, along with details on this limited edition machine. Since then some helpful correspondents sent me reams of historical data on the Fair. So in this edition I want to supplement what I wrote earlier.

The 1933-34 World's Fair was officially named the "Century of Progress International Exposition". Its Century of Progress theme was chosen to celebrate the centennial year of Chicago's incorporation as a village (1833). Private investors funded the World's Fair, and original plans were for it to be open for one year. However, not all investors had been repaid by its planned closing in October 1933. So the Fair reopened in April of 1934 and continued until the end of October. Attendance was very good, 22 million and 17 million in the two years respectively. Net, the investors finally made some profit. However, the Fair's major impact was in helping to shake off the "Depression blues" as it was termed by social historians.

Just why did *Singer* choose to "officially introduce" its new Model 221 *Featherweight* sewing machine at this Fair? I think there were two reasons. First, simply that the *Featherweight* design was perfected in the timeframe immediately preceding the Fair. It was already being sold. Here was a chance to showcase it to untold millions of women! Second, the design was a giant leap forward from the heavy and ungainly sewing machines of the past - and it fit in perfectly with the theme of the Exposition. A Fair booklet stated that Manager Hubert Burnham and his Commission were actively seeking examples of "Progress through science and its applications". Chevrolet even had an assembly line at the Fair where cars could be ordered one day and delivered on the following one. So, is it any wonder that *Singer* decided to show its progressive *Featherweight*!

Are all of the very earliest *Featherweights* the Century of Progress edition? The short answer is no. Although the "official introduction" of the Model 221 was at the Chicago World's Fair, readers will recall that the machine had been manufactured since mid-1933 and was being marketed across the country, not only in Chicago and at the Fair. However, the 1934 Century of Progress limited edition must be one of the most historically significant variations of the Perfect Portable. I'd love to have one in my collection.

1936 Texas Centennial Exposition Featherweight (also see page 66)
The 1933-34 World's Fair in Chicago was popular and thought to be financially successful, although in reality the profit was only modest. Our country was coming out of the Great Depression and attendance and sales showed it. Civic leaders in Texas saw an opportunity to reapply the Fair concept to their upcoming state Centennial in 1936, celebrating 100 years of independence from Mexico. The Texas Centennial

Commission was authorized by a constitutional amendment and members were chosen in mid-1934. They were tasked with putting on an equivalent event in less than two years. Dallas was chosen as the primary site, with a smaller one at Fort Worth. Donald Nelson, who was involved in the Chicago World's Fair, became the Commission's Chief Designer. The 1936 Texas Centennial Exposition opened on June 6, 1936, at what is now called the "State Fair Grounds". The Commission met its objective although attendance was short of expectations. During its six-month showing the Exposition in Dallas hosted over 6.3 million visitors, but lost money because of the major capital expenditures for construction. However, the Greater Texas and Pan-American Exposition that followed in 1937 attracted even more visitors and allowed some of the loss to be regained.

1936 Texas Medallion

Julie A. York

With this historical background you can imagine how the *Singer Sewing Machine Company* saw another opportunity for "hands on" demonstration and sales of its products to countless women who would be there. Considering the number of visitors, a special *Featherweight* medallion was created; this would enable Model 221 buyers to leave the Exposition with a memento of their visit.

I am thankful to Julie York of Idaho who supplied this photo. She owns the Texas Centennial Exposition *Featherweight*, serial number AE 077472, that originally belonged to her grandmother. Julie wrote that she is "very happy to be a part of owning a bit of history".

I am not sure how many Texas Centennial Exposition machines were made. There were over 6.3 million visitors at the main Exposition at Dallas and almost one million to the Fair at Fort Worth. But how many bought *Featherweights?* Over the past ten years I've received over 1000 letters from correspondents and only four of them refer to the Texas machine. Nothing can be extrapolated from this data, but I'll stick by my earlier statement that they have to be rare. An educated guess is they would number in the hundreds.

Black Crinkle Finish 221 - the Model 221 SV 1 (also see page 67 - 70)

Since writing about the curious black crinkle-finish *Featherweight* I've received just a few more letters from folks who were delighted to discover they own one. A letter from Marilyn Moodie in California is a typical one. She wrote that she bought hers six years earlier "in a dingy little Sewing and Vacuum Shop in San Francisco. I was a Feather-weight neophyte at the time and only wanted a small machine to use as a backup and to take to class. There was also a shiny Featherweight for sale but I opted for the one with the crinkle finish because it was $50.00 less expensive than the other. It is only since then that I've learned that this model is quite rare. So, all in all, I'm very happy with my little machine. And knowing that there just aren't many around like it makes it even dearer to my heart". Marilyn's machine is serial number AF 387907, from the first production run. She made a wise choice on that day in San Francisco. A friend who buys and sells *Featherweights* told me she heard of one that sold for $3200. last year!

A most interesting letter came from Wayne Arnold in Texas who owned (at the time) a black crinkle *Featherweight*, serial number AF 589499, with the regular circa-1947 shiny striated faceplate - not the crinkle finished one with vertical grooves. Wayne included a copy of *Singer's* inspection ticket that accompanied all new machines. This ticket clearly shows the machines' serial number, and that the black crinkle Featherweight was designated as the Model 221 SV 1. The machine was purchased new in 1941 at Oyster Bay, Louisiana, and is currently owned by Gail Pickens-Barger of Texas.

I also heard from several "old salts" who were stationed aboard Navy warships during and just after World War Two. One explained that true to naval tradition, they still had a sail locker aboard - even though sails were long gone - and a small black sewing machine was kept there to mend hammocks. He told me it was just like his wife's *Featherweight* but had a rougher finish. Another seaman repaired

Gail Pickens-Barger

Model 221 SV-1

clothes on a Light Cruiser and he signed out a black crinkle machine when the ship was decommissioned in the early 1950's. He brought the machine home and his wife used it for many years. It was recently sold to a collector for $2000. With this data, I continue to believe that the black crinkle *Featherweight* originated as a federal contract version, most likely for the U.S. Navy. It seems logical that the naval service machines were from the first production run in 1939. Later, after the war, what was probably an over-run of the special grooved machine beds were assembled with a mix of pre and post-war parts, designated the Model 221 SV 1, and sold on the commercial market. These later machines will have serial numbers in the AF 589200-600 range and will generally be found with the shiny striated faceplate.

While on this subject let me warn *Featherweight* collectors that it's possible to create a counterfeit black crinkle machine. All that's required is to repaint a regular *Featherweight* using the special crinkle-finish paint that's available from auto and machinery supply sources, and to apply the *Singer* decals on its sewing light and machine arm. A professional could do it, and cheat a casual buyer and history. Readers should note that a genuine black crinkle machine will <u>always</u> be a series AF machine and will <u>always</u> have two parallel sets of grooves cast into the machine bed and swinging bed extension. Check carefully before you buy a spurious machine and make a costly mistake.

Blackside Machines (also see pages 70 - 73)

A *Featherweight* variation that's near and dear to my heart is the so-called "blackside" machine. Whenever I see one I think of our country's tremendous wartime efforts and the immense sacrifices of our parents and grandparents. The blackside made very limited use of shiny nickel or chromium plating. The clouds of World War Two were gathering and both metals were especially needed for production of machinery and military ordnance. Even aluminum (machine beds) and copper (motors and wiring) became critical items. *Singer* worked under this constraint in the months preceding the conflict, and even tried to build its inventory as a hedge against U. S. involvement in the war. Later, civilian production was stopped as the company swung to defense production. The War Production Board had finally intervened. All Family Sewing Machines in stock at Elizabethport were frozen and allocated for use by Government agencies. During the war years *Singer* even advertised in women's magazines and newspapers, offering to buy "idle Singers" from people to help ease the crunch caused by the scarcity of sewing machines.

I've had an interesting litany of correspondence on the "blackside" *Featherweights*. In the earlier edition I stated that the earliest one I knew of was AG 011747, owned by a woman in New York. Just after the book was printed a Maryland couple wrote telling me they own its barely older twin, serial number AG 011746. Later, a correspondent in California reported blackside AG 011600. Then, a woman in Iowa told me she owns serial number AG 011004. This is almost 2400 machines earlier than the AG 013403 *Featherweight* owned by a couple in Michigan. Two years went by and I didn't hear any earlier serial numbers so I thought that was it. But then a man from California called to report serial number AG 010249, manufactured on 2/10/41 as per *Singer's* records. By coincidence, within a few days I received a letter from a woman in Maryland who said she owns a blackside "that might add to your store of knowledge". She bought it second hand in the mid-1960's in Connecticut and used it to make her wedding dress in 1976. Its face plate, presser foot and lever, hand wheel rim and several of the attachments are all finished in black. Her machine is serial number AG 009623.

As I write this in 2001 I haven't heard of any earlier or later pre-war blacksides, so I did my math again. It would appear that almost 3800 machines exist between the earliest and latest serial numbers reported for the pre-war version of the blackside *Featherweight*. So, the range of serial numbers of these desirable machines has expanded, and it may expand again as additional examples come to light. However 3800 or so machines is a fairly small number considering the total production of *Featherweights*. They are still a "very limited edition" with immense historic significance.

I also wrote about some later blacksides that were sold after the war, and included a photo in the second edition. This version is essentially the same as the earlier one - with limited chrome/nickel trim. But it has a black pressed steel face plate in place of the blackened scrollwork one. The one in the lower photo on page 72 appeared to have a teardrop head retaining screw for its faceplate. I questioned the teardrop shape at the time because it seemed like an overly complicated piece to manufacture, but was fooled by the angle of the photo. Actually, the presser foot lever is raised and an illusion is created which makes the round head of the screw appear like a teardrop. Unfortunately, no additional examples of this machine have come to my attention. Right now I'm at three and counting. There has to be more of these post-war machines out there.

"Made in U.S.A" Featherweights

Some of the black Model 221's made at Elizabethport have a "Made in U.S.A." marking under the machine medallion. I received a few reports on these machines just after the last edition was complete and I tracked some down to verify the special legend. Every one I'm aware of is in the AF series that was made in 1941 prior to our country's involvement in World War Two. Likely explanation? I believe these *Featherweights* were made at Elizabethport for export - to help fill the pipeline for Model 221's that was formerly supplied by the Clydebank factory in Scotland. Clydebank was promptly engaged in war work after the British entered the war in 1939. As time went on the manufacture of civilian goods was restricted and shipping from Great Britain became more difficult. Apparently *Singer's* management tried to ease the world's demand by supplying from the U.S. Earlier, there was no need to mark the Elizabethport machines with the special legend because very few if any were exported. Is the "Made in U.S.A." marking a guarantee that your machine was exported during this historic time frame? No, I don't

"Made in USA" Medallion

Patricia A. Williams

think so. I have creditable reports from owners who bought their new U.S.A. marked machine at the *Singer* store in Hometown, U.S.A. during the war years. Apparently they were exported and sold domestically during the same time frame.

Singer Medical Instrument (also see page 70)

My second edition referenced a medical instrument designed by *Singer* that used a *Featherweight* bobbin. I didn't have any documentation on it but only a sketch from a collector in Michigan, who told me the instrument was used to sew up wounds in combat. Since then I learned that the Summer 1943 edition of McCall's Needlework had an article on the "magic needle" as battlefield surgeons called it. It said that the new Singer Surgical Stitching Instrument was developed after twelve years of research and that it is "one of the greatest contributions to medical science today". The magic needle enabled the surgeon to complete suturing without assistance and reduced the time required by 75%. Some further research revealed that it was widely used on the home front as well as in the military. *Singer* had supplied them to a small group of influential surgeons in various specialties; they in turn used the instrument as a prototype and later endorsed it when it proved out. The "magic needle" was promoted by a group of specially trained demonstrators and was widely shown at medical conventions and hospitals. Unfortunately, I could not find any mention of the sterilizing procedure!

Singer Centennial Model - British Machines (also see pages 75 - 76)

When I wrote about this model last time, every single one of the British Centennial *Featherweights* I'd seen had its light switch on the end of the light fixture. This is unlike the Centennial version made in the U.S. with the switch on top of the machine bed. However, since then

205

I've learned that they were made both ways. A woman in Iowa has a 221K Centennial, EF 560919, with the light switch on the machine bed. Also, a correspondent in Australia owns two: EF 917567 with the machine bed location, and EG 708945 with the switch on the right end of the light fixture. And a woman in Nevada has the very latest British Centennial *Featherweight* I'm currently aware of - EG 710987. Its switch is on top of the machine bed. From these and other reports I've concluded that the light switch was generally on the machine bed on earlier Centennial British machines, perhaps to about the end of the EF series. Then, with the EG series the switch could be found intermixed in either location. Why this is, I do not know. Suffice it to say, though, that either location is proper and original. *Featherweight* enthusiasts and collectors shouldn't fret if their machine is a few serial numbers away from one that is documented with a different type of light switch.

State Fair Machines

Over the last few years I'd heard rumors of special edition *Featherweights* that were sold at State Fairs. But I had never seen one. Frank and I had leads on two of them but we came to dead ends when one owner passed away and another one moved. But then a good friend put

1954 Texas State Fair Medallion

Fred A. Switzer

me on to a genuine 1954 Texas State Fair machine that's owned by Fred and Barbara Switzer in Texas. I learned that the Texas State Fair is held annually in Dallas, same site as its Centennial event in 1936. While researching, I could hardly wait for the photos to arrive! Theirs is a striated face plate Model 221 machine, with serial number AL 546374. Its birthdate is late 1953. The medallion does not have a raised surface as on regular *Featherweights* of that vintage. Instead, it is smooth to the touch. This suggests a very small production run that would not justify the expense of a special stamping die. The machine was purchased by the current owners in the state, and was in home use as late as the year 2000.

How many Texas State Fair *Featherweights* were made is not known. I've heard that about six of them are in the hands of collectors. I am not sure if they are all 1954 Fair machines, or possibly other years. My contact in Texas spoke with a retired Singer District Manager who told him that the company tried the concept of using state fairs to increase sales. He remembered that the 1954 date coincided with a large sales promotion by the company. Are there more out there? Well, I'm sure there is - at least the Texas State Fair version. It's hard to believe that less than a dozen machines were manufactured with a special medallion. Possibly the state fair concept was tried in other states. Just think, the next time you spy a *Featherweight* in its black case with a "For Sale" sign, it might have a medallion that's a bit different than the one you expect to find!

1964-65 World's Fair Featherweight

There is some evidence that a white-colored 221K7 *Featherweight* was made to commemorate the 1964-65 World's Fair held in New York City. I mention it here because I've heard from several people who attended the Fair and saw them on display. But despite some extensive sleuthing I haven't been able to get my hands on one as yet.

I had a lead a while back from a woman who's uncle was a District Manager with *Singer*, retiring in the mid-sixties. He owned a *Feather-weight* that was supposedly purchased at the 1933-34 Chicago World's Fair, but the machine is a white-colored 221K7 that wasn't made until the 1960's. I thought it might be a simple mistake; possibly it was really linked to the 1964-65 World's Fair, not the one in the thirties. I wrote for more information. Unfortunately, the machine does not have any special markings that might differentiate it from any other white-colored 221K7 machine. So there is no way of documenting it. Another person wrote to me about a "white 1964 World's Fair machine that's the center-piece of my collection". The comment was included in a long letter along with many other tidbits. It took me a while to catalog it and when I wrote back for more information my letter was returned, because the sender had moved and the mail forwarding notice was expired. Then, just recently I learned that a reputable collector in California owned one. But his reply said he sold it a long time ago. However he did relate from memory that the machine had a silver/orange medallion with "1964-1965 New York World's Fair" and a reference to the Singer Building on it.

All told, I believe there's ample evidence to continue searching for a New York World's Fair *Featherweight*. Hopefully one or two will surface in the future. This is another Model 221 I'd really like to see.

Magnesium Featherweights (also see page 81)

One of the legends that linger on and on is that some of the post-war *Featherweights* were made of magnesium instead of aluminum, turning it into an "Ultra-Featherweight" sewing machine. Magnesium is only about two-thirds as heavy as aluminum but it's rarely used in its pure form. So, assuming a magnesium alloy was used for its machine bed and swinging bed extension, such a *Featherweight* would weigh about two pounds less than its regular aluminum counterpart. I continue to receive letters reporting the existence of these machines, but I've never been able to see one or even to get a serial number.

I speculated earlier that the so-called magnesium *Featherweight Model 221* might be a machine marketed by the White Sewing Machine Company, and called its "Featherweight Portable Type in the Luggage Case". This was the White Model 77MG. Its MG model number designation and the chemical symbol for magnesium (Mg) were just too similar to ignore. A casual observer could easily mistake it for a genuine *Singer Featherweight*; it looked similar, was advertised as a "Featherweight" and had a black luggage type carrying case. Eugene Zacharias from Maryland sent me a photo of one, serial number 77MG-60245. Apparently they were made in fair numbers. He and his wife purchased it new in California in 1950. While Mr. Zacharias was serving in the Marine Corps at its El Toro Air Station, his new wife found out that the "winter there was not quite as mild as she had expected". So she said, "I want a new sewing machine and then I am buying some flannel and making myself some proper night clothes". They went to the local *Singer* store but the dealership did not offer a military discount, hence the visit to White and their 77MG.

Author's Note: the White77MG was also finished in a green color. A man in New Mexico sent me photos of one that was a wedding present to his wife in December 1948. Their daughter in Texas currently owns it. I was especially interested in this because the White 77MG was advertised as "The Featherweight Portable Type" and it is green. Could this be one of the origins of the legend of the green-colored *Singer Featherweight*?

Eugene F. Zacharias

White Model 77 MG

Then there is the Domestic Sewmachine, Model 759-153MG. I have an undated brochure that shows one. It says the machine is "The famed Portable! Full size but light-weight (due to the use of magnesium)". It too looked like a *Featherweight* but the similarity of this machine with the White 77MG shown above was remarkable. I did some research. Domestic was bought out by the White Sewing Machine Company in 1924 and was operated as a somewhat independent subsidiary until the Great Depression. Thereafter, White used Domestic as a brand name. No wonder they looked like twins!

So there you have it…. at least two small portable machines that look like *Featherweights* and use magnesium in their construction to achieve light weight. I think we can safely say that the jury is in. The legend comes from these and possibly other machines. The *Singer Featherweight Model 221* was never made out of magnesium.

Red-colored Featherweight (also see pages 82 - 83)

Last year Frank was with me at the Quilt market in Houston and he talked with a well-known vendor who related a story he'd heard several times on the circuit. A woman had a *Featherweight* that had a lot of surface wear. Her husband owned an auto body shop. She asked him to repaint the machine to make it look better. When he asked what color, she said "red". He thought she was serious and when he returned with the machine it was bright red. The machine was displayed in a local shop for a while where it caused many comments by customers.

I don't know if this story is factual but it does underscore the old saying about one look being worth a thousand words. Let's say it is true. How many people would have walked away having seen a red-colored *Singer Featherweight?* And how many would have told their friends or mentioned it at a quilt guild meeting? Then, sooner or later, it becomes the absolutely original red *Featherweight.* The information finally hits the Internet and collectors scurry to find the machine, with enough money for a queen's ransom to entice its owner to sell.

I still believe that the red *Featherweight* legend is the result of confusion with *Singer's* red-colored miniature sewing machine that was called its Model 20 Sew Handy. Although I continue to receive letters about red-colored Model 221's, I've never been able to get one in my hands to examine. I was off teaching a couple of years ago when Frank took a call from an excited woman who had just found a red-colored *Featherweight* at a pawnshop in New Jersey. She asked him if it was worth $800.00. A few questions later he determined that it did have some wear and tear on the paint, but she didn't remember seeing any *Singer* decals on the sewing light, the machine arm or its bed. He told her he thought it was probably a repainted machine that was used for a while after the painting, or was artificially "aged" to make it look like it was used. She was going to go back to the shop to inspect it more closely and ask more questions. We never heard from her again.

Just as with the black crinkle machine, it's possible for a skilled craftsman to create a counterfeit red (green, blue or whatever) *Featherweight.* And it would fool most buyers. Painting has become pretty sophisticated and replacement machine decals are available from aftermarket suppliers. Collectors beware! Always insist on documentation before buying anything other than a recognized machine edition.

All told, when it comes to repainting I still think an original machine should be left original, no matter how badly its finish is worn. I've received photos of Model 221 machines that were repainted in all sorts of colors - raspberry and candy-apple red included - with no intent to deceive anyone or to create anything other than a display piece. Oftentimes, the rationale is that the machine is badly worn and the owner is saving it from being "parted out". But I just can't understand this. The machine, just like each of us, has earned those nicks, scratches and wear marks. It's a piece of history.

Musty Odor (also see pages 94 - 96)

One of the most common complaints I hear from *Featherweight* owners is the musty odor that lingers in some of the carrying cases. It's more noticeable with machines that were stored away for years or decades, compared to those that received regular use. My earlier edition covered this topic in detail and there's no need to review the same material here. I did have an interesting call though, from a man in Montana, who proposed that the smell is the result of old motor grease that has turned rancid - rather than from mildew in the fabric lining of the carrying cases. He told me that mildew is very uncommon in his section of the state, but his carrying case still has the musty smell.

This explanation sounded plausible so I returned to my microbiologist friend. He explained that the growth of mildew, and how fats and oils turn rancid, are both biological activities. And the occurrence of either (or both) in an enclosed space like a carrying case will result in the smell permeating the fabric of the case whenever the machine is stored in it.

The remedy I use remains the same. I still haven't found anything better than what I call the perfume strategy, using several sheets of Bounce fabric softener in the bottom of all my cases.

Vinyl Carrying Case

In 1998 I was lecturing in Waco, Texas and a woman brought her *Featherweight* to class in a bowling ball-type bag that was marked *Singer* on a metal plaque on its front. The bag fit the *Featherweight* perfectly and it had internal straps like hosiery garters to hold the machine in place. The bag was beige outside and black inside, and was made of a vinyl like material. Unfortunately, I didn't have a camera with me so I was unable to get a photo of this bag. Whether it was designed as an accessory specifically for the *Featherweight* machine, or was original to her machine, I do not know. Possibly it was made for a later model *Singer* portable. It is the only one I have ever seen.

Later that same year I began a long correspondence with Diane Anderson of Ontario, Canada, who owns a different vinyl carrying case for her 221K7 *Featherweight* machine, serial number FA 226089. Her machine is the regular Clydebank Scottish machine, white in color. The carrying case is turquoise, with an interior of tan and a heavy sheet of clear plastic sewn over the bottom. The inside of the case is reinforced on all sides and doubly so on its bottom. The case does not have the *Singer* name or logo on it, and the only markings are on the latch/lock device, which is marked "HOMA" and "Swiss made". The case is about 13" wide by 10-1/2" high and 8-1/2" deep, with four rounded chrome plated feet on its bottom. It has no trays or clamps inside for tools or accessories. Diane told me the woman who owned it previously had assured her that the carrying case was original to the machine and that her daughter bought the set when she was in college.

Turquoise Carrying Case

After seeing the soft case while in Texas, this information whetted my interest. I began to look at the carrying cases women used to transport their machines to class. Most of the ones I saw were the original hard cases as supplied by *Singer*. Once in a while I noticed regular bowling ball bags that were adopted when the hard case was missing or broken. I also saw a variety of the modern nylon soft cases that are available currently... but nothing in the way of a soft case that looked like it might be original to the *Featherweight*-manufacturing era. Then, later that year some sleuthing by Diane Anderson turned up another turquoise carrying case almost identical to the one she owns, except that the latch has the word "TOURING" on it. A woman in Halifax, N.S. owns this case. Diane also related that she talked with a man in Toronto who is a *Featherweight* and antique sewing machine collector. He told her that some years before he was offered a white 221K7 with the identical vinyl carrying case, but the machine was in poor condition and the price was too high, so he passed.

These reports were encouraging but I was still a bit skeptical about the authenticity of the turquoise "soft carrying case". It certainly appeared to fit the *Featherweight* to a "T" but the lack of the *Singer* or *Simanco* trademark was troubling. I did some research on the name HOMA and learned that the Homa Lock Company is currently a leading distributor of locks and specialty hardware, supplying components to manufacturers of sewn cases for many years. The company has offices in the U.S. and Canada and gets its components from many countries. I speculated that the carrying case manufacturer probably used HOMA locks because they were readily available in the commercial supply channels.

Two years went by. I continued looking for turquoise carrying cases on my quilt lecture and teaching travels but didn't find any in the U.S. But additional research and correspondence led me to locate several more examples of this soft case in Canada or with owners who obtained them from Canada. They were usually accompanied with a white 221K7 machine. I was getting closer to recognizing its authenticity as a genuine *Singer* product from Canada, because there were just too many examples to ignore. The final word came from Diane Anderson who originally brought the turquoise case to my attention. She spoke with a former executive who worked for Singer-Canada in the mid-1960's. He was in the *Singer* office in Ontario that was also a warehousing location for machines and accessories. He remembered that the vinyl *Featherweight* cases arrived from Quebec in large cardboard boxes totally labeled in French. Unfortunately, he did not recall the name of the company but did remember that *Singer* had contracted with it and that it was located near the Canadian factory at St. Johns, P.Q. He also recalled that *Singer* promoted the fact that the vinyl cases were very rugged, with cardboard molded into the vinyl in the bottom. Reportedly, the turquoise cases were referred to as "totes" in a (circa) mid-sixties parts book from Singer Canada.

All told, I believe the turquoise soft carrying case is a genuine *Singer* accessory. It appears to be a proprietary Singer-Canada product, only sold in Canada, which accounts for its scarcity in the states. I would love to have one in my collection. But so far, I haven't found one that is for sale!

Featherweight Card Tables (also see pages 100 - 104)
In the first and second editions of this book I showcased the famous "Folding Utility Table" (usually called the Card Table) as the scarce and desirable *Featherweight* accessory that it is. Since then I've received many letters and comments from folks who found one at an auction or antique store where the seller had no idea it was anything but a folding-leg table with a curious removable insert in its top. Another common tale is how the buyer found one at an outdoors flea market where the dealer was using it as a display table. Thankfully all the "new owners" will save these bits of Americana from further wear and abuse. I've even received photos of regular, modern card tables that were cleverly adapted to hold a *Featherweight* machine flush with the top. Some of them look really good and they will undoubtedly serve their owners well.

Readers will recall there were two models of the Card Table, the Models 308 and 312, roughly corresponding to the pre and post-war eras. They used different mechanisms to hold the removable insert in place when the table was used for something other than sewing. There were several variations including wooden and metal edge trim, also wooden and metal legs. The different manufacturing conventions suggest multiple factories. So far I've documented *Singer* cabinetworks in South Bend, Indiana, and Thurso, Quebec.

I thought I'd seen it all but Mary Abbott from Ohio brought another one to my attention. She owns a Card Table that is very similar to the Model 312. Its hardware is clearly stamped with the *Simanco* trademark, and the table and insert are match-marked with serial number T 046207. However, the insert design is odd. Its sides are straight and parallel with each other, and the one side <u>does not</u> have the change of width "jog" to accommodate the Model 221 machine base. Also, the insert does not extend all the way to the edge of the table, but ends 3-4" away. There is a L-shaped "bulge" at that end. None of her *Featherweights* fit this Card Table.

Unidentified Singer Card Table

Mary L. Abbott

So what is it? I suspect it's a Card Table that was made for another *Singer* machine model. Hopefully, additional examples will come to light in the future so we can positively identify this one. Meanwhile, though, *Featherweight* enthusiasts should positively identify the correct Card Table for a Model 221 before buying one at a premium price. A Card Table made for the *Featherweight* will have a jog (or change of width) along one of the long sides of its removable insert. Therefore, one that has straight sides will be suspect. If you are unsure, try fitting a Model 221 machine in the opening before making the buy.

Reduced-size Card Tables

A correspondent in Iowa brought an interesting *Featherweight* Utility Table to my attention. She owns one that is only 19" wide. When it is folded the legs stick out and make it awkward for storage; but she writes that it "sure is handy in my sewing room". She bought the table from a local antique dealer and really doesn't know anything about its history. Her husband did carpentry work for over 50 years and he inspected it, comparing with a regular Card Table she owns. He said that if the table was cut down, a real craftsman did it - because its corner bevels match, likewise with the edge moldings, and the leg mechanisms work like they should. Later she found a former *Singer* store employee who explained that in Iowa at least, "if they were really trying to sell a machine and a table, and the lady said the card table wouldn't fit where she wanted to put the machine, that they would offer to cut the table down for her". She cautioned me that she didn't know if the story was true or not, but was just repeating it verbatim.

I do not believe that *Singer* ever manufactured anything but the regular 30" by 30" Model 308 and 312 Card Tables. Making a smaller table for sewing in tight quarters just doesn't fit with the concept that it could be used as an auxiliary table for other needs in the home. Besides, why make a rectangular one that has legs sticking out when the table was folded? No doubt the 19" Folding Table in Iowa is a regular *Singer* Card Table that was cut down by a craftsman for a specialty need. I agree that it would make a splendid sewing table for smaller work. Possibly there are more like it out there. Just be aware that it cannot be documented as a genuine *Singer* factory product, so if you find one the purchase price should be reduced accordingly.

Cost

I have often been asked what Card Tables cost when they were new. Many people bought theirs along with a *Featherweight* machine in a "package deal". A woman from Wisconsin sent me a copy of the sales slip that was in the carrying case with her AH series machine. The slip shows that the machine and a Model 312 Card Table with serial number C 768281 were purchased in Oshkosh in August of 1949 for $173.00. Some other documentation I have indicates that the Model 312 Card Tables sold for about $40.00 alone, sometimes less and other times a bit more. Apparently the Sewing Centers had some pricing flexibility. I don't have any reliable data on the pricing of the earlier Model 308

Utility Table at this time. They probably sold for a bit less when they were made.

Card Table Covers

When World War Two began in September 1939, *Singer* sewing machines were sold at some 2000 retail Sewing Centers throughout the U.S. Gradually and then more quickly, the company became involved in vital war work, with the result that many of these Centers closed their doors due to the lack of sewing machine stock for civilian sales. The Company did what it could to keep the remaining stores open and a "Fashion Services Department" was created to expand the sewing articles and notions women could expect to find in *Singer* shops. Despite great difficulties with material shortages, items such as sewing and service gift boxes, aprons, scarfs, hankies, boudoir boxes, and Snuggle Doll kits were offered to help retailers make a go during the tough times. Another two of these wartime items were the bridge table cover, and the "special cover for the Singer Utility Table". A Christmas 1943-dated *Singer* advertising brochure in my collection advertises the special covers for the Card Table in water repellent rayon moiré for only $2.00! From what I can tell from the black and white brochure, the cover had a motif with large and small flowers. I would imagine that the cover had elastic on its corners to hold it in place. Undoubtedly most of them have long since been worn out and discarded. But maybe I'll get one of these covers some day…. a true *Featherweight* lover just has to have hope!

Motor grease (also see pages 111 - 112)

For normal use *Singer* recommends refilling the motor grease tubes at 6 to 12 months intervals. If you have a *Featherweight* that hasn't had its motor lubricated in eons, don't put it off any longer! Oftentimes the old grease has thickened up and it's difficult to refill the tubes. If this has happened to your motor, try using a straightened paper clip or even a toothpick to help remove the hard exposed grease. Remember that the proper grease is *Singer's* part number 190613. It comes in a convenient plastic tube, although I'm still told it's hard to find in some areas.

THIRD EDITION ACKNOWLEDGEMENTS

Mary L. Abbott, OH; Diane and Doug Anderson, ON; Wayne K. Arnold, TX; Leigh Ausband, SC; Sandra Barrett, BC; Larry and Sandra Byrd, MD; P. Gaylord Cascio, MD; Charlene Drewry, NV; Denise Erbacher, Australia; E.R. Hannah, BC; Susan Leftwich, TX; William R. Lyle, IL; Peggy A. McBride, IA; Shirley McElderry, IA; Marilyn Moodie, CA; Anne Morgan, N.Z.; Dale G. Niewoehner, ND; Deloris Pickens, OK; Gail Pickens-Barger, TX; Carolyn Powers, CA; Rick Rann, IL; James Slaten, CA; Lorraine Smith, WI; Fred A. Switzer, TX; Gloria Torrieri, PA; Patti Williams, CA; Helmut Wolf, NM; Julie A. York, ID; Eugene Zacharias, MD

PERSONAL MACHINE DIARY

MODEL NO.	SERIAL NO.	PURCHASE INFORMATION

EPILOGUE

Through all three editions of this book I have tried to gently stir a better appreciation for the wonderful *Featherweight Model 221* in the minds and hearts of users and collectors alike. And through this Supplement I hope I've added a few more points of knowledge on the Perfect Portable to each of you. If I have succeeded at either or both these goals, then the labor in researching and writing, plus my delight in doing it, will be its own reward. More than this no writer can expect.

The many who are fortunate enough to own a *Featherweight* sewing machine possess a true American treasure. Most are still whirring away in sewing rooms and seminars across the country, others are valued for their comparative rarity and they enjoy "collector status". Treat them with honor and love. Without a doubt, they are symbols of the last generation of American craftsmanship!

Nancy Johnson-Srebro

ABOUT THE AUTHOR

Nancy Johnson-Srebro is an internationally known quilt teacher, lecturer and show judge. A prolific author, some of the books Nancy has written include... *Measure the Possibilities with Omnigrid®, Endless Possibilities using NO-FAIL® Methods, Rotary Magic, Block Magic, Block Magic, Too!, and Stars by Magic.* An upcoming quilting book with C&T Publishing, Inc. will be released in 2006.

Mowry Photo

Nancy's works and methods have become standards for rotary cutting and precision piecing of quilts. And her first edition of the *Featherweight* book (1992) helped this wonderful machine become better known and appreciated around the world. She lectures and teaches extensively, sharing her love of quiltmaking and the *Featherweight 221* sewing machine with quilters across the country.

HER HUSBAND

Francis J. Srebro was a Department Manager with the Procter & Gamble Paper Products Company. He was born and raised in northeastern Pennsylvania and was strongly influenced in his early years toward mechanics and the Sciences. Frank was educated by the Jesuits and he worked part-time as a machinist while in college. Before his retirement, he had mechanical, environmental and engineering management responsibilities over most of his career with P & G. This background serves him well to understand and appreciate the mechanics and functions of the *Featherweight* sewing machine.

Nancy and Frank are the proud parents of three children - Mark, Alan and Karen. They are blessed with a wonderful granddaughter, Casey Tyler Srebro.